MIRACLES IN THE AUSSIE BUSH

The Des Miers Story

Shelley & Jeff Reaney

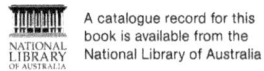 A catalogue record for this book is available from the National Library of Australia

Miracles in the Aussie Bush
Copyright 2025 ©Shelley & Jeff Reaney

Published by Star Label Publishing
P.O. Box 1511, Buderim, QLD, Australia
publishing@starlabel.com.au

All Scripture references are from the New King James Bible unless stated otherwise.

All rights reserved. No part of this publication may be reproduced in any form; stored in a retrieval system; or transmitted; or used in any other form; or by any other means without prior written permission of the publisher (except for brief quotes for the purpose of review or promotion).

The views expressed here-in remain the sole responsibility of the author, who exempts the publisher from all liability. The author and publisher do not assume responsibility for any loss, damage, or disruption caused by the contents, errors or omissions, whether such contents, errors, or omissions result from opinion, negligence, accident, or any other cause, and hereby disclaim any and all liability to any party.

ISBN: 978-1-7637645-3-8

Foreword

The Bible says that nothing is impossible with God[1] and from firsthand accounts I know that God does what is impossible in our natural world. I have experienced His amazing interventions, miracles and healings in my and my family's life on so many occasions that I wanted to record them. Biggest ever thank you to Shelley and Jeff for their work in bringing my dream for a book to reality.

Some people reading this may think that I have made up or exaggerated the stories, however, to the best of my recollections, the events happened as stated. In most cases, my dear wife, Ada, was a witness to the miracles that happened.

I am a bit hazy on exact dates. There is a dividing line though at January 1981 ... before we knew Jesus and after we came to know Him.

It is my hope and prayer that the stories bring glory to God – my Healer, my Saviour, my Master. This narrative is not about me or my family primarily, it's about the goodness and love of God towards us.

Desmond Miers 2024
Gympie, Queensland, Australia

---

1 Luke 1:37

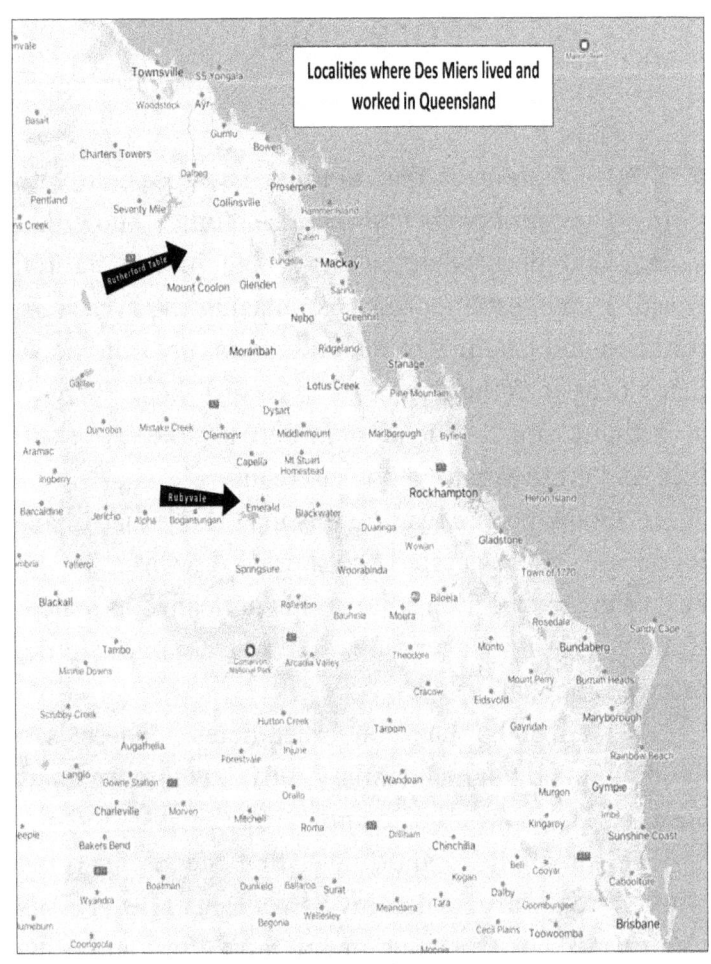

Source: https://mapcarta.com/Central_Queensland

Chapter 1

In the late 1970s my wife, Ada, our adult son, Greg and I operated a gold mine from an isolated camp at Rutherford Table in central-western Queensland. We were situated around 150 kilometres southwest of the coastal town of Bowen, with the nearest civilisation sixty-five kilometres almost due south at the mining ghost town of Mt Coolon. The township consisted of one house and one hotel which functioned also as the Post Office, petrol station and news agency ... total population was four people.

In time for Christmas 1980 we drove 1,825 kilometres south to Sydney, New South Wales, to see Ada's ailing mum, Patricia, known affectionately as Nan by relatives, neighbours and friends, fully expecting that it would be the last time we would be together. In her late seventies, Nan had endured ill health for many years; she suffered with high blood pressure and sugar diabetes and had survived two strokes. She also had a serious heart condition which required daily medication, an ankle injury, and several other ailments. As the tyres thrummed on the bitumen and we chewed up the distance to Sydney, our thoughts coincided, *Will we get there in time to see her before she goes?*

Finally, we arrived at the family home in suburban Doonside. As was her habit, Nan was sitting on the veranda. She leaped out of her chair and ran down the stairs to greet us. Astonished, I blurted to Ada, "She looks fifteen years younger!" This was not what we had expected; she was full of life! Although one of Ada's sisters had already told us that Nan had 'gone all religious' this was far from what we had anticipated. During the next fortnight, her fascinating story unfolded. Nan had been incapacitated to such an extent that she received Meals on Wheels.[2] One day her only son, Cyril, took her to a church service at Penrith Christian Fellowship.[3] She hobbled into the church. Even though she had proclaimed, "nothing can heal me," Cyril continued over the next four months to take his mother to healing meetings. God had plans for Nan and in that time, she received numerous miracles, being healed

---
[2] Meals on Wheels is a government-sponsored organisation that provides meals delivered to people's homes by volunteers if the recipients are incapable of preparing meals for themselves.
[3] Now known as Imagine Nations Church Penrith, New South Wales.

completely of many sicknesses and infirmities. She was perfectly well, took no medication and bubbled over with joy and new life. We were stunned by the evidence of what God can do when someone puts their trust in the Lord Jesus Christ and the power of the Holy Spirit.

Nan, Ada's mother

At Christmas time Nan took us to one of the church meetings and it was so different from the church that I knew as a kid. At one point the pastor stopped preaching and said, "Oh, there is someone here with a dreadful hate." I knew that he was talking about me, and I wanted to crawl under the chair! He didn't ask that anyone acknowledge this, but we knew then that God was real and having seen the evidence of Nan's healings, both

Ada and I wanted healing for our bodies. We determined to find out more about this amazing power.

My carefree childhood in Alberton, south-east Queensland was shattered by the death of my Mum when I was six years old. After that, my Dad, Alf, worked in Brisbane, the state capital, milking cows at night so fresh milk was available the following day. I saw him only once or twice a year, and then just for one day each time. I was raised first by my grandparents, then an uncle and aunt. Those were miserable years. At the useful age of around eight years old I worked on the farm, so I missed school regularly. Sometimes I was belted with a piece of firewood to prevent me from going to school. When I was forced on Sundays to go to Sunday School, I felt it was so unfair that half my day off was taken up with religion. Fifty years later I realised the value of Biblical teaching which encourages the training of children to have faith in God while they are young because it will stay with them as they grow older.[4]

---

[4] Proverbs 2:6

My religious upbringing took place in the Lutheran Church, attended by all the local folk of Prussian descent, like me, but we were never taught about salvation.[5] With three others, I undertook Confirmation. We received instruction about the doctrines of the Lutheran Church and sat exams, just like at school. One Sunday morning when the church leaders thought we were ready, we were brought before the whole congregation and were asked a lot of questions about the Bible. I don't remember not passing.

I left school when I was thirteen-and-a-half (nobody said I couldn't) to cut my uncle's sugar cane for ten shillings[6] a week and my keep. When I was fourteen after an altercation one night when he had belted me, I'd had enough of his abuse, and left home on my pushbike. I sought help from the local publican who knew my uncle well! Through his contacts I was offered a job loading bunches of bananas onto horse-drawn wagons. I worked there for a couple of weeks and then Dad invited me to Brisbane to work on his fruit and vegetable delivery run. I stayed with Dad for a

---
[5] Salvation is the cornerstone of the Christian faith and entails a person putting their faith in the finished work of Jesus to cleanse them of sin, save them from Hell, heal their body, and restore their relationship with God the Father.
[6] Equivalent to one dollar – in today's money that would be about forty dollars.

couple of years, working six days a week. Sunday was a workday too as I had to mix concrete for the foundations of his new house in Taringa. I wasn't happy about not having any free time, nor spending all my time with a dad whom I didn't really know.

You can take the boy out of the bush, but you can't take the bush out of the boy. I searched for a way out of my situation and found that one of Dad's customers had connections to a land surveyor who worked in the outback, near Cunnamulla, 750 kilometres west of Brisbane. He was a good man and I worked well with him. We subdivided sheep stations[7] for government land grants to soldiers returning from overseas war duty.[8] At sixteen years old, I was the lead chainman and axe man. If there were any trees in the way of the line, regardless of their size, they had to be cleared and I was just the man for it. I worked with the company for a couple of years and when the job finished, I went to Charleville because there was a certain young lady there.

---

7 Large grazing properties where livestock are raised for wool and meat.
8 Second World War.

Des, aged 17 at Tibooburra Station, west of Charleville, Queensland.

Then seventeen, I accepted a short-term job west of Charleville on a sheep station with my cousin, Ron. The job stretched from a couple of months to over six, with workdays from daylight till dark. I must have done a good job because the station owner gave me a bonus! His brother at Uardry Station[9] near Hay in central New South Wales needed a man to work in the merino stud and I was offered the job along with a free flight to Hay, with a stopover in Sydney for ten days at a private hotel at Potts Point.

This offer came out of the blue and I had to make a tough decision as I was somewhat attached to that certain young lady in Charleville. Should I go or stay? There was plenty of work in the area (as was everywhere in those days) and my cousin lived there too. I couldn't make a decision, so I tossed a coin! I parted company with the young lady and headed south with a bonus in my pocket and a holiday in Sydney to boot. I had a wonderful time and then flew to Hay. I didn't have any indication that God was involved in my life but He was setting up a rendezvous.

---

9   Uardry Station (known originally as Wardry) is a 34,618 hectare pastoral lease that operated as a sheep and cattle station in New South Wales from 1840. Carrying about 25,000 sheep and 1,000 cattle, Uardry was recognised for a very long time as one of Australia's most prestigious Merino studs. Situated about forty kilometres east of Hay and south-west of Griffith, the Station has a 32-kilometre Murrumbidgee River frontage in flat plains saltbush country. Uardry was sold in 2012 to Tom and Patricia Brinkworth, one of Australia's biggest woolgrowers, owning more than one million hectares of land across New South Wales and South Australia, and 350,000 sheep. The Uardry sale price was in the vicinity of $30 million. However, within weeks of the purchase, Tom Brinkworth sold the 18,000 stud Merinos and restocked with 18,000 head of cattle moved 2,000km from the Northern Territory in one of Australia's largest cattle drives. He died in 2020 at age 83.

No one was there to meet me, and after a long wait, I called the Station as night was falling. They had forgotten me, so by the time we arrived at Uardry it was dinner time. I saw about twenty people in the dining room and then this good-looking woman walked in.

That night I met the love of my life! It seems the Lord had His hand on Ada and me from way back ...

Ada had worked picking fruit in Leeton and became friends with another girl. When the season ended just before Christmas they searched for jobs via the newspaper classified advertisements.

Uardry Station near Hay, 170 kilometres away appealed as they were both looking for adventure and a change of scene. Ada's friend worked in the laundry and Ada served the jackaroos[10] in the dining room.

---
10 A jackaroo is a man (usually young) who is learning the work of a sheep or cattle station.

The Uardry Station homestead

One Saturday, bored with routine, Ada and her friend were on the lookout for entertainment, as there wasn't any at the Station. Ada's money had almost run out because wages were paid irregularly but she wanted to go to the Carrathool Hotel[11] for the Saturday night dinner and dance (how she loved dancing!) She had noticed me on the men's quarters' veranda that afternoon and hoping that I might be flush, sent another guy over to ask if she could borrow some money.

I thought, *this is my opportunity! If I'm going to help them have a good time, I'm not going to miss out; I'm going, too!* Five of us went to the hotel that night; three riding in the back seat. We had only a few drinks but on the way home, we discovered our driver must have had one too many. We were in unfenced open sheep

---
11 A distance of about 14 kilometres.

country, with wide, rough roads and stock grids that indicated boundary lines. The grids were marked with three logs embedded vertically in the ground each side. Suddenly, the car swerved and slid sideways across a grid and hit one of the upright logs which brought us to a sudden halt. Fortunately, we weren't travelling very fast, but something had broken in the steering and the car wasn't drivable. We couldn't expect help from other drivers, as cars were infrequent on that road, especially at night. So, we had to walk home. The driver, perhaps too drunk to move, the other guy and Ada's friend stayed with the car. After walking for a while, Ada was thirsty and found a puddle on the side of the road, so she got down and drank from it. She said that it was the best drink she'd ever had. Eventually, we arrived back at Uardry. That was the start of our romance.

The original Carrathool Hotel, established in 1873 was destroyed by fire in 2010. A new hotel was built and opened in 2015.

Chapter 2

We had to work the next day, despite being weary and it being Sunday. I was always on call, being the nursemaid to twenty stud sheep. And the jackaroos needed to eat, so Ada had to work that day too. As nursemaid to the rams, among other jobs I trimmed toenails, stirred and changed straw bedding, and watched the clouds for rain, in which case I would bring the rams into the shed. They were VERY pampered animals. There was only one other man working with me; the leading hand/manager, so it was full-on work most of the time. A Uardry ram was depicted on the Australian one-shilling coin in 1941 and back in those days one ram sold at the Sydney Royal Show for £4,000. In today's money that would be $332,000!

We lived at the Uardry main station with twenty to thirty people, while the outstation had forty men who were employed in eradicating rabbits, which were in plague

1941 Australian one-shilling coin

proportions. One night we were invited to the rabbit camp to play penny poker, and later I hauled home our winnings.

Ada was so good at bluffing the players, one of the ploys of the game, that they never invited her back.

A couple of studs!

Ada, in Sydney aged 17 or 18

On our days off, we went fishing in the Murrumbidgee River, which flowed behind the Station. We caught Murray Cod that weighed a few kilograms each. We used to row down the river and walk in the bush, as there was nothing else to do. Naturally, I was seeing Ada every day. Transport anywhere was a problem but there was a railway siding at Uardry so we took the train to Hay a few times. It's quite a distance, about forty kilometres.

When the rams had been pampered and prettied up for sale, another lot of twenty would be brought in for the same treatment. After about ten months, with the different batches coming and going and doing the same thing over and over, I found the work boring. Ada wasn't very happy with her work, either. Somewhere along the way I popped the question and asked her to marry me, but her answer was a forgone conclusion as we both knew we wanted to be married! There wasn't any couples' accommodation available so we set off to Ada's mother, Nan, in Sydney.

On the way, we stopped at Leeton, booked a motel for a few days and visited Ada's older sister and her husband who lived about ten kilometres out of town. My future brother-in-law asked about our plans once we arrived in Sydney, saying that work around Leeton was plentiful. He knew a farmer up the road who was looking for a man; and a house came with the job. The work was tractor-driving on the wide-open spaces at Stoney Point.

Where to get married presented a problem. We didn't have much financially, nor could Nan help fund a wedding and my Dad and step-mother were over a thousand kilometres away. It became too hard to plan around these issues, so we decided to get married in Leeton. Therefore, Ada's brother-in-law took us to the farmer and I got the job. He wanted me to start work straight away, as he needed to harvest peas for the cannery. I said I needed a few days before I could start. Our free house, although it wasn't luxurious by any means, did have electricity.

I asked Ada about her denomination, and she said Presbyterian, so we went to a pastor in the town and told him our story; he said he'd be happy to marry us. We set a date for our wedding within a couple of days. Ada had befriended a couple of ladies at the motel, and they agreed to be our witnesses. Unfortunately, our brother-in-law couldn't attend due to his work commitments and Ada's sister didn't drive; however, everything else just fitted together conveniently.

Our wedding day, Leeton

Ada had a blue suit and decided to wear that for our wedding, which wasn't anything special; we were in love and just wanted to get married and make it all legal. We were married on a Monday morning, a very hot and windy day. That afternoon, we went downtown to a second-hand shop and bought various pieces of furniture and other essentials. We found a man with a truck to transport our goods and it was almost dark when he finished the delivery. We managed in one afternoon to get everything, including food supplies. We spent a couple of days setting up house. That was our honeymoon.

On the first few days of my new job, I stood on the back of a big truck and pitchforked complete pea bushes full of pea pods into a two-metre-high stack, then onto a conveyor belt which dumped the bushes into another truck for transporting to the cannery. I have no idea how the cannery separated the peas from the bushes! Then followed a lot of tractor work, both inside and outside the channelled irrigation area, around and around, day in and day out. It was boring at times.

Ada remembers that we had our first argument in that little house. She packed a bag planning to go home to her mother, however, when I saw that it was MY suitcase on the bed, I said she couldn't go if she was taking my case. So, what could she do, but stay!

The house was only forty-five centimetres off the ground with one or two steps up. One day I came home and was shocked to see that a black snake had slithered up the stairs. At first, I didn't realise it was dead. Ada had managed to kill it by throwing a shovel at it! She's not afraid of snakes and has dealt with quite a few when they've invaded her territory.

Our first home, Leeton

The economic times were good with lots of work so I could pick and choose my jobs. I was offered one at an orchard close by and at better pay with a better house. While I worked there our daughter, Shelley, was born. When the day came my boss took Ada to the hospital. In those days I only had a push bike, so after work I rode to visit Ada in hospital which was about a twenty-kilometre round trip. After a week we brought home a beautiful baby girl. Nan came to stay for a while to help Ada and to spend time with her other daughter. We could catch a ride on the school bus, or our relatives would take us to Leeton.

Ada and Shelley at Leeton

Working in the orchard went well; mainly in a team, picking oranges, apricots and peaches. Also, I drove a horse and wagon to carry picking boxes to the pickers and collected the full boxes late in the day. After the evening meal, I helped the boss grade the fruit until about 10.00-11.00pm, and then loaded it onto a truck. The farmer would leave in the truck at 3.00am to get an early place in the queue at the cannery. Working hours were long but the money was good. Winter was pruning time and that was a lousy job. Leeton gets cold in winter. On my own, standing on a ladder in the fog, pruning peach trees with the dew dripping down my arms ... all day long ... in the cold. I felt like I was the only one left in the world. All the fruit work was seasonal, and most of the year I had plenty to do, but it was different in the off-season. During those times, I worked on a nice little vegetable garden I had started at the front of our house.

Other work was available, including fencing, and working on the rice headers during harvest. I had acquired a motor bike and, as the orchardist had put me off for a while, I could travel to a rice farm. The bike was the old type with a sprung frame, but it didn't like corrugated roads and one morning it threw me. I lost the sleeve off my leather coat and a bit of pride, but I didn't have any injuries, thank God.

Although we liked our second home, the boss turned the work on and off like a tap. While looking for another house we found a Model T Ford,[12] the last model ever made. At the time, wheat farmers were troubled with kangaroos grazing on the new crop, so I went

---

[12] The last Model T was produced in 1927. The production of the Model T made car ownership achievable for many people. It was easy to maintain, simple, sturdy, versatile, had interchangeable parts, and was virtually unchanged throughout its 19-year production run. Henry Ford said of it: "It had stamina and power. It was the car that ran before there were good roads to run on."

'roo shooting with a few chaps in the Model T. The local police heard about it, and they joined us. The vehicle was unregistered, and I didn't have a driving licence. One dark night as I was driving in gullied[13] terrain outside the main rice irrigation area with the police guys standing on the running board, I had to hit the brakes and they went airborne over the mudguards. That upset their applecart for the night. They knew I drove the Model T to get to work and warned that they'd have to book me if I drove an unregistered vehicle up the main street. Down the track I decided to get a licence, so my brother-in-law took me to the police station. The officer took one look at me and wrote out the licence. He knew I could drive!

A spruced-up 1927 Model T Ford; a lot better-looking than the one we owned!

---

13 A gully or ditch is formed by running water cutting into the soil on a hillside.

Once a month we went with half-a-dozen friends to shoot wild ducks on the rice fields. The following night the six families would gather for a party, and each shared what they had shot the previous evening. There was always a certain amount of beer on hand. Shelley slept through all the noise and when the party was over, she'd wake up. Some nights, Ada and I drove the Model T to the orchardist's farm and trapped rabbits. Shelley was cosied up in the back. We'd snooze too, while we waited for the traps to be sprung. We'd gut the rabbits and then take them to my brother-in-law, who sold them for me to the Narrandera meat works.

We'd had the Model T for a while when a rental house became available. However, it was a step backwards, as its condition wasn't as good as the house we had and it wasn't wired for electricity. It meant though, that I could look for full-time work and pick my jobs.

Our second home, Leeton

Ada, Des, Greg and Shelley at Leeton

Around this time Greg was born; he was a good baby. Ada had to do all the washing by hand, though.

I did all sorts of casual work at the Leeton Irrigation Department and then later was put on full-time. This meant about a ten-kilometre daily trip. At first, I worked with a team cementing water channels. It was hard work, but the pay was good. I soon graduated and worked alongside the workshop, repairing tyre punctures, greasing and washing vehicles, and tidying up the irrigation bailiffs' new Holden utilities. Every morning I'd have about half a dozen tyres to repair, from all types of vehicles – tractors, cars, trucks, whatever.

Shelley aged 3, and Greg about 18 months old

We saw an ad in the paper for a share house with an old lady in Yanko, which was closer to town. It was a nice place, but she was odd. She impatiently waited for my arrival every afternoon so she could tell me about the children's behaviour, both good and bad. As we shared the house, we ate our meals together and as she sat at the end of the table, she would slap it continuously with a carving knife in a sort of threatening way. We thought we had better leave. As Nan wanted us to go to Sydney, which had been our original plan, I swapped three dozen rabbit traps for a 1927 Whippet (like a Model T Ford) and trailer. I needed to fix the oil pressure on the vehicle, but it meant, thankfully, we were able to say goodbye to the old lady. I don't remember what happened to that old Model T.

We set off for Sydney and camped under the bridge at Gundagai on the first night. I can't imagine how we managed to sleep overnight with two children in the Whippet, but we did. The next morning, we forgot to remove the baby's nappies that Ada had washed, pegged out and left to dry on the trailer. They were dry at our next stop! We blew a tyre about a hundred kilometres outside Sydney, which meant we didn't have a spare from then on and roads were rough in those days. After our arrival there was a big reunion with Nan and the family.

Another brother-in-law knew what was going on around town and through him I was able to get a job at the local brickworks not far from Nan's place. Tiles were pressed out of clay, and we had to wheelbarrow them along a dirt track (which should have been concreted) to twenty kilns for firing. Frequently, there'd be rubble on the track and if a barrow hit the rubble, it would tip over. I dropped a barrow twice in one day, and, in frustration, told the boss what he could do with the job and walked out. Fortunately, I'd been paid the day before. I came home from a new job one day and learned that the boss from the brickworks wanted me back. They had concreted the track.

I had found a better job assembling refrigerators at St Mary's, but the boss was replaced and I wasn't happy about that, so I left and worked at Chief Clothing in Blacktown. It had good management, manufactured shirts of good quality, and it was a good job. I was on a line of seven men doing the pressing, with a daily quota of 150 shirts each. Within three days I was pressing my quota and then learned there were bonuses if we did more. It was a race! We ended up earning three days' pay in one day. I stayed there for a few years; however, I developed asthma brought on by nervous tension and inhalation of toxic fumes from steaming new materials.

Chapter 3

We bought a property at Marsden Park, about fifty kilometres north-west of Sydney, and started a little farm on good ground. Ada did a lot of the work growing tomatoes, and later, orange trees. Shelley and Greg started school there. Someone introduced me to selling Street's ice cream out of a van, with the vehicle and all equipment supplied. I had a designated area and travelled around in the van, ringing a bell to let people know I was in the street. Payment was a percentage of whatever was sold. I rang that bell every weekend for quite some time.

Eventually, I gave away the clothing company job and sold ice cream three days a week, which worked out fine. I also sold cakes, biscuits, lollies, and tobacco. It was like a corner store on wheels. No beer, though!

A fellow who lived near us asked if I was interested in cutting the timber on his land. He and I felled the trees and I split them into blocks, posts, and firewood. A large firewood merchant said he'd take whatever I could produce, which created a bit of pressure, because we had to ensure that we had a load ready for him whenever he arrived. In between times, I built a shed, and we lived in that rather than a caravan. Another enterprise emerged when we found a big patch of maidenhair fern growing in the bush near Windsor so, via a contact we had, we sold potted maidenhair ferns to Woolworths. You wouldn't get away with that these days!

**Marsden Park
"Had to start somewhere!"**

Ada and her tomato patch

Despite my childhood experience, we sent our children to Sunday school. The pastor had been a kangaroo shooter until his conversion to the Lord Jesus Christ, and later started leading a church. He sold his brand-new car to fund the restoration of the church's roof when he began ministering there. He was a down-to-earth person and it wasn't hard to respect him. The only time we went to church though, was at Christmas time for the children's concert.

Greg and Shelley – Guy Fawkes Night

About that time, Dad told me that his brother, Harold, wanted to sell his shack on ten hectares of land at Alberton in Queensland. Ada and I were very keen to leave Sydney, so I headed north to see what was on offer. Uncle Harold had been brought up on the land, then when he moved to Brisbane, he wanted something to do on weekends other than to mow lawns. He had used the Alberton property only for weekend fishing trips, although he had installed a few beehives. He took me to see the neglected hives located towards the front of the property and told me not to be fearful. However, when he lifted the lid, he ran. They were as wild as hornets because he had never worked them.

I used to tell Ada about Queensland's mud crabs and mangoes, and we wanted some of that as soon as possible. Dad was also interested in buying the block, but I was the one who did the deal and paid Uncle Harold seven hundred and fifty pounds for it. Converted to today's money that would be about thirty-one thousand dollars.

To enable us to get organised to sell our property in Marsden Park, Shelley and Greg were sent north to Ada's sister's farm at Nabiac for a few months. We made three trips north to Alberton moving our stuff and collected the children on the last trip through. We finally arrived in Queensland on Shelley's birthday in June 1960.

The block at Alberton hadn't been farmed nor was there any equipment, just the shack on lovely river frontage, plenty of bush and a huge mango tree. Despite the hardship of my childhood,

I dreamed of being a farmer. We had to clear land again in preparation for crops. Dad even convinced me to buy a draught horse for ploughing. To keep bread on the table I also worked for the local shire council. On Sundays our children went to the Alberton Lutheran Church, however, Ada and I didn't attend.

Uncle Harold's fishing shack at Alberton and Dad's (Alf's) fruit truck

For the family's first experience of a mud crab meal, I made a crab pot, baited it and put the pot in the water at Jacob's Well. We caught a few beauties and cooked them over an open fire. We didn't take anything else to eat; we just went there to get our dinner. Crabs are not as plentiful now.

I then put crab pots in the river at our farm. We caught so many that we kept them with mangrove leaves in chaff bags marked Monday,

Tuesday, Wednesday, etc. so that we knew in which order to cook them. Shelley and Greg often had crab legs for their after-school snacks.

Our first home at Alberton; later we added an extension

One of Dad's brothers-in-law, Reg, gave me work spraying the ever-present weeds on his riverbank. Regular floods spread a wide variety of undesirable plants that never could be controlled successfully. We were growing corn which he had also grown for his cows and when he offered his corn cobs to us, we sold them at the market. When we were struggling to make ends meet, Uncle Reg and Auntie Ivy were a real help and blessing to us. When I was a boy my first Christmas stocking came from them. Of my ten aunties and uncles[14] she was the best and I had a very soft spot for her.

We decided to grow strawberries for the Brisbane market. I'd heard it said that if you want

---
14 My Dad's siblings

to grow anything, grow a luxury item, and we felt strawberries were the way to go. We bought our first strawberry plants from a local man. It was hard work but worth it financially. That was the start of better days for us.

Who doesn't love strawberries?

At our most productive time we had 21,000 plants and had so much fruit we paid up to five workers to do the back-breaking harvesting work. Ada would pack the berries all day into presentation boxes for the fresh market, and whatever was left over at the end of the day had to be stemmed for cordial production by the Golden Circle cannery. I feel sorry about how often our children had to pull berry stems late into the night, even on school days.

We delivered the strawberries before midnight to the carrier's pick-up point which was a locked shed beside the road, past the Gem Hotel at Alberton. Some nights we couldn't make the deadline because we had an abundance of fruit to prepare so I had to be the delivery man. I'd work all day, sleep two hours, load the utility, drive to the old Roma Street Market in Brisbane, an eighty-kilometre round trip, drop off the fruit, return home, sleep two hours and then drive back to Beenleigh (20km return) to pick up the workers for the day.

When we trialled increasing our sales by sending two-kilogram presentation boxes of strawberries to the market, an agent came to ask if I could increase the supply, as he wanted to air freight the produce to the Adelaide Market. Our top sellers though were the single-layer flat presentation boxes with our best, tasty fruit. We were paid three pence, which now equates to over eighty cents, per strawberry for that fruit. In between seasons, on the river flat ground we grew corn, potatoes, cabbages, cucumbers, peas, tomatoes, sweet potatoes and capsicums; however the latter were prone to disease, so we stopped growing them.

One day, while we were crabbing at Jacob's Well, we saw a huge black cloud in Alberton's direction. We arrived home to find we'd been hit by a massive hailstorm. The whole of our apple cucumber crop, due for picking, had been wiped out. That setback, along with insufficient water on the property for irrigation and unreliable rain, was the tipping point that led us to give up farming.

During one off-season I was offered a job building pigpens which included a lot of cementing work. When I wasn't building, I looked after and fed the pigs for the employer. He sold out and I took one sow in lieu of a week's pay. We'd had her only a few days when she presented us with a litter of twelve! So, I had to build a bigger pigpen. That's how we got started with our own piggery. We still didn't know God personally, but He was providing for us in every situation.

Around that time, we sought to connect to the electricity grid; we had generated our own power up until then. However, it was too costly to have it brought onto our property. We saw the potential for developing a piggery, so we sold the farm and bought an eight-hectare block which had roads on all four sides at what is now 191 Rotary Park Road, just up the road from our first

Alberton property. The block had been owned long ago by one of the families who owned the Gem Hotel. There were various fruit trees, but no river frontage from which to catch crabs.

Uncle Reg put in a word for me with the Beenleigh Shire Council and I started there laying water pipes around the Woodridge housing development. I worked my way up to driving a front-end loader. On our new block we lived in a caravan until we could build Ada's dream home and at night I built a storage shed. In hindsight, I have no idea how I managed to survive the heavy workload of my day job, shifting properties, and building two sheds: one for the growing pigs, and then moving them.

Council lent me a front-end loader and I cleared the land at the front of our block and hired a bulldozer to level it so I could put down the foundations for our house. We had a motorised concrete mixer, which I used to lay the cement floor. We dug sand and gravel at Jacob's Well and carted it home in a trailer so we could make our own type of Besser bricks (rock block). We bought a brick mould to shape the bricks which were 200 x 380 millimetres. While I was at work, Ada mixed loads of concrete, packed it into the mould, then removed the wet bricks from the mould and left them to dry on a long bench. She made about thirty each day; I have no idea how many in total. Someone was so impressed with her work that they bought some from her.

Des and Ada with their new house taking shape

Meanwhile, the pigs were in temporary buildings, so I applied for a permit to build a piggery for thirty breeding sows. About the same time, we had the opportunity to pull down old houses that were being cleared for a new housing estate at Bethania and take the building materials for use in building our pens. We built slatted floors in the piggery so that pig waste would fall underneath and be available for methane gas production. Later, we planned to generate the power to heat the piggery in winter. We developed our herd up to twenty-five breeding sows which meant a lot of little pigs! We sold the young suckling pigs at eight weeks old and topped the markets with their quality. We were making good progress until dry weather arrived which turned into drought; nobody had feed, so no one wanted to buy pigs. Broken hearted, we sold our good breeding sows to the abattoir for meat.

Around this time Ada wanted a pressure cooker. A wheeler-dealer from Norwell had one (his wife's!) and he sold it to me against her wishes. Sometime down the track he asked Greg to go with him to the sapphire fields in central Queensland, which explains how he always had money, and Greg came back after a week with a wad of notes. Greg became very interested in sapphires. In the meantime, a huge hailstorm caused awful damage right throughout the south-eastern area of Queensland where we lived. When it occurred, I was right in the middle of it in a Council truck at Woodridge; a terrible experience I'll never forget. The hail damaged metal roofs across the area but insurance covered the repairs. Opportunity knocked; I bought a stack of slightly damaged roofing for our house at a rock bottom price. I had to hire a semi-trailer to get the materials home. Shelley at thirteen, dreaming of a future in architecture, designed the plan for our home. It had a big central courtyard garden walled-in with glass on three sides. She left the farm for the bright lights of Brisbane when she was seventeen while Greg stayed with us and worked for a neighbour at one time, along with other local jobs.

We had just built our house to lock-up stage when Greg returned from his second trip to the gem fields with our wheeler-dealer friend, and another wad of notes. Christmas was around the corner and our friend asked us to join him in Rubyvale, nine hundred and sixty kilometres away. We were overdue for a holiday, so drove to our Sydney family for a week, and then returned and went to Rubyvale. Conditions were primitive and it was as hot as hell living in a tent in the stifling heat. Although we found some sapphires Ada wanted out of that hellhole as fast as possible and never return. Greg went back with our friend another time and came home with another pile of money. I had itchy feet and was sold on the idea of moving to Rubyvale, as mining gemstones appeared to be a lot more profitable than working for the Council.

Chapter 4

Greg and I talked incessantly about the possibilities of sapphire mining and eventually, Ada came around to our point of view, and asked, "When are we going?" She didn't want to stop Greg and I and knew she couldn't stay there on her own.

Ada was sad about leaving the house, as she had poured her heart and soul and a lot of hard work into making all the bricks for her dream home. As it turned out, many years passed before she lived in a real house again.

Alberton house at lock-up stage was designed by our 13-year-old daughter, Shelley.

One of our brothers-in-law came along at the right time and we gave him the job of caretaking at Alberton. He and his wife and daughter lived in the caravans and did the gardening. We went to Rubyvale, returned to Alberton only occasionally, and, without any reason to keep the property, we eventually sold it. Our relatives moved out and we took the caravans and set ourselves up at Rubyvale. We worked with our wheeler-dealer friend in his mine. One third of whatever we dug went to him and we kept two thirds. Our costs came out of our share.

Ada and Des sapphire mining at Rubyvale

We worked from eight in the morning until dark. We'd eat and then go back to work until midnight. The sound of the motors running our equipment nearly drove the neighbour nuts. The weight of our first parcel of sold sapphires was 850 grams. It was a good mine and the stones just kept rolling in. Both Greg and I did the digging in the mine and moved the dirt along a little railway line to the shaft. Amongst many other jobs, Ada washed the stones. We worked for our friend for about six months.

I started using a divining stick[15] to find sapphires and close to our friend's mine I found another good run of stones which we pegged for ourselves. We hired a guy with a drilling rig to bore a 122 centimetre-wide hole to a depth of about 10-12 metres on that claim. We built the ladders out of 2.5 centimetre agricultural piping. We built our own equipment so that we could wash the stones out of the gravel that we mined.

Ada became a film star when we were working for our friend. She had to stand on a platform several metres off the ground to release the gravel from a huge bucket into the washing equipment. Tourists used to stop and take photos of her while she worked.

---

15 After we became Christians, I stopped using the divining stick because I was unsure whether that kind of activity would please the Lord. Later, I learned the Bible is very clear that God forbids the practice.

Ada, the film star!

We had two caravans, a tent, a hut with a wood stove, an overhead water tank and a canopy made from a parachute over the top of it all, so in the smallest breeze it would flap and give us some cool air. The picture of our camp (next page) taken by an unknown photographer, was reproduced as a postcard and sold to tourists at our local shop. Like us, the other prospectors camped wherever they wanted, and the whole area looked like a shanty town.

We found another spot near our camp, staked a claim, and drilled another bore hole. On the first day, we dug out a large yellow sapphire and sold it for $1,000. The yellows are the most precious of all. We only had one duffer of a bore hole, right under our camp; the stone was too scattered to make the effort profitable.

Occasionally, we went to Bundaberg for a few weeks of rest but couldn't be away for very long, as prospectors are obligated to work their claims five days a week. There was always the possibility that someone would take over the claim if it wasn't being worked. I didn't hear of anyone actually doing that during our time there, though stories abounded, and with severe consequences.

Our camp at Rubyvale. This photograph was reproduced as a postcard for sale to tourists.

One of Ada's younger sisters and her husband, with their two boys, came to visit one time and worked our mine while we travelled further outback to explore for opals. However, we didn't see enough to convince us to move away from sapphires.

We depended on buyers from Thailand to buy our sapphires, as the local buyer didn't pay what they were worth. We always took our best stones to Bundaberg or Brisbane to get better prices. With one Brisbane buyer we used to swap our stones for mud crabs. The Thai buyers would pay $100 per ounce (28 grams) for our low-grade stones. They would bring Thai university students out to the fields to act as interpreters. However, we learned later that they could all speak English.

City girl Shelley, having a Rubyvale adventure.

Dad and my stepmother also came up once and even went down the mine. We gave Dad a lady's jackhammer so he could look the part in front of the camera.

Several things happened around that time which, in hindsight after we were saved, showed us that we had an enemy who had been at work attempting to bring trouble and even destroy us.

On one occasion, we drove a Landcruiser with a very overloaded trailer from Alberton to Rubyvale and Greg followed us in his vehicle. At Miriam Vale a wheel came off the trailer which caused our vehicle to flip and land on its side off the road. We managed to crawl out unscathed through the windscreen and were amazed that a twenty-litre drum of petrol on the roof of the Landcruiser hadn't exploded, nor had a crankshaft moved that was stowed behind the back seat. We had packed well, and only lost the bottled milk and Christmas cake from Nan, Ada's mother. The police allowed us to drive our vehicle with a badly dented roof to Rockhampton for repairs.

Another time, while driving a Ford Falcon station wagon and towing an empty trailer over the mountain range on the old road between Mackay and Marlborough, there was a huge thump underneath the car. Greg stuck his head out of the window and saw the back wheel of the car, still attached to the axle, but outside the mudguard! On this Ford model there was only one master cylinder for the four wheels, so when the brake cylinder on that wheel popped out, the brake fluid in the braking system poured out and drained from the other wheels too, so we had no brakes and no gears.

At this stage the road passed through a cutting with rock walls on either side; we were at low speed and fortunately, no other cars were on the road. I spied a gap in the rock wall facing uphill on the other side of the road from where trucks had carted road-building gravel, and as our speed increased, wrenched the steering wheel hard to head our vehicle into the gap. As we went through the gap up the slope the vehicle slowed and then rolled backwards, so I jack-knifed the trailer against the car which brought us to a standstill. If that gap hadn't been in the wall, there was nowhere else for us to go except down the long steep hill – with no brakes and no gears. It could have been the end for us. We carried out some temporary repairs on the vehicle to enable us to drive, ever so cautiously, to Rockhampton for repairs and to buy a second master cylinder so that we would never face something like that again.

On another occasion, we were on our way from Rockhampton to Rubyvale with a loaded trailer. It was late in the day with light rain. The road was narrow bitumen and passing cars had to straddle both the bitumen and gravel on the side of the road, which was probably about eight centimetres lower than the bitumen. It was dangerous driving at any time because the change from bitumen to gravel could rip tyres to shreds. We were the last of six vehicles following each other at a reasonable distance, all doing the speed limit, when an oncoming vehicle with a horse float appeared and he wanted all the road! The front driver didn't move over onto the gravel either, causing the horse float to clip the side of his car. What followed was mayhem, with the cars behind going in all directions. It all happened so fast, but

I remember seeing that we were headed straight for a vehicle that was crossways on the road. I wrenched the steering wheel and broadsided down the bitumen and gravel, sprayed mud and gravel over the vehicle in front of me and barely missed him as we headed off the road into a water-table gutter about a metre below road level. As it had been raining for some time, there was water and long grass, but somehow, and I can only say, miraculously, I was able to control our car for the whole length of the vehicle chaos on the road. We landed at the head of the line of cars on the bitumen, right way up, trailer and goods intact and ready to go again. Praise God! Amazingly, no one was injured, but the driver who'd been in front of me sure had a mess to clean off his car.

At Rubyvale, we were allowed to have only ten horsepower of site power, so we bought an alternator from an old gold miner who lived outside Collinsville, 400 kilometres north of us. Sometime later, he turned up at Rubyvale and asked if we would be interested in working his gold mine at Rutherford Table, which was south of the proposed Burdekin Dam. We checked out his mine and found it to be profitable, even though the old miner's colourful character was questionable.

By this time, we had been at Rubyvale for six years of hard and hot work with not much time off. The sapphire buyers had stopped coming to the gem fields, necessitating that we go to Bundaberg and Brisbane to sell our stones. Also, we had obtained a mining homestead lease, which required that we put improvements on the land within twelve months. We, including our son Greg, were happy to leave it all behind. We sold out to eager buyers and moved to Rutherford Table to try our hand at mining gold.

Around that time, I saw an article in the local paper about Pastor Clark Taylor[16] who was holding healing meetings in Townsville and Bowen. I'd suffered with stomach ulcers for a long time and planned to go, however, the Bowen River flooded which prevented us from getting there. He later returned to Bowen, and we attended a meeting. That was the first healing meeting I'd ever been to; I convinced myself that

---
16   Clark Taylor converted to Christ at a Billy Graham Crusade in 1959, founded the Christian Outreach Centre (COC) in Brisbane in 1974 and established many other churches and an evangelistic TV program, preaching healing and miracles, which aired throughout Australia in the 1980's. COC later renamed to International Network of Churches (INC).

I was just checking it all out. Although I didn't ask for prayer that night, I was surprised at how positive I felt about that possibility. Perhaps that meeting prepared me a little for what we encountered on our visit to Nan for Christmas in 1980.[17]

---

17 Recounted at the beginning of Chapter 1.

Chapter 5

Our move from Rubyvale was huge. Using our truck, we made four trips to Rutherford Table transporting all our belongings and equipment, including a little Fiat bulldozer that we'd found and bought in pieces and reconstructed from a manual written in Italian. We couldn't understand the words, so we rebuilt it from the diagrams and drawings. On the first trip Greg stayed to set things up at our new camp, which was located seventy kilometres from Collinsville. The gravel roads between Rubyvale and Rutherford Table presented many challenges for a large vehicle. We were full of hope at the prospect of our new venture, although starting over again with a massive workload ahead.

The mine shaft was twenty-seven metres deep, bored by a big drill. The old miner's equipment was unsatisfactory, so we replaced it with ours. Greg did the digging at the gold face about thirty metres underground, and about a hundred metres into the hill. He loaded the dirt into a little trolley on a railway line which ran to the base of the shaft, where Ada shovelled the dirt into smaller buckets, loading about four metres of dirt in three hours. I winched the buckets to the top of the mine and ran them on a railway line to the truck, which was parked part-way up the side of the hill, but at a lower level than where we were. After the bucket came up, all going well, the dirt would end up in the truck. Sometimes it didn't! We then trucked it to the washing plant, which Ada controlled. Working conditions in the mine were pleasant in the summer, being about twenty-one degrees Centigrade. We mined the dirt, washed it, and gave the old miner his share of the findings, which slipped through his fingers as fast as he got it.

The move to Rutherford Table

When we realised that we'd mined up to the edge of his lease, with his permission we pegged a lease alongside his. Later, after finishing with the mine, we started open-cut work. To complement our Fiat bulldozer, we bought a tractor and then found a D8-size bulldozer broken down on the side of a road. We searched out the owner, bought it, put it back together at the roadside and Greg drove it seventy kilometres cross-country to camp. By this stage, we had pegged ten to twelve claims, each being about ninety square metres per claim.

Moving the Atco units

There was a gold-mining company about five kilometres away from where we had our leases. I had bulldozed a lot of dirt for them and in return, they were to cart dirt for us, but they didn't come through with their part of the agreement. Not long afterwards, they went broke and left their claim and equipment sitting in the bush. As we wanted three of the twelve-metre Atco units, known as dongas and used for temporary housing, and some of their machinery, we offered to be caretakers, providing we could shift the units to our area. Eventually, we kept the units and some equipment, and thus profited by that company's demise. We used two of the units to house casual workers and guests, and the other became our dining and lounge room.

We had noticed for some time a dragline[18] standing at the side of the road. It was left over from roadworks; apparently too difficult for the contractor to move. Again, we found out who owned it and sang them a song for it! However, this machine couldn't be driven cross-country and it cost us more to get it home than to buy it. We used it to clean out our slurry ponds.[19]

---

18 Heavy-duty excavator.
19 Excavated large ponds which held our mining waste.

We used the dragline to build the dam and slurry ponds.

Greg and Des at the gold wash 'race'.

We built all the washing plant works.

Ada working our first wash of gold dirt at Rutherford Table.

Tipping dirt from the mine.

Chapter 6

After saying our goodbyes to 'miracle' Nan in Sydney in early January 1981 we headed north, reflecting all the way back to Queensland on what we had seen and heard. We called in to see Dad in Brisbane and searched out the church to which people in Sydney had referred us, Christian Outreach Centre.[20] On Sunday morning, 11 January we attended the service and received the Lord Jesus Christ as our Saviour. The people of the church were so alive and it was so good to be there that we went back that night. "Twice in one day!" I exclaimed. We had changed instantly and dramatically; we were 'born again' and would never be the same! That night we were filled with the Holy Spirit and I spoke a few words in another language that I did not know. I don't remember anyone explaining this to me but I felt that I was praising the Lord. I learned later from Mark 16:17 where Jesus instructed His disciples: "And these signs will follow those who believe: In

---
20 Now Citipointe Church Brisbane with numerous locations across Australia, New Zealand, Europe and the USA.

My name they will cast out demons; they will speak with new tongues."

Passing through Mackay Ada noticed a building that had been a picture theatre but now advertised itself as 'New-Way Outreach Ministries' and underneath that was a sign twenty metres long and one metre high for all the world to see, 'NOTHING IS IMPOSSIBLE WITH GOD'. That sounded like it might be the sort of church for which we were looking. After making enquiries there we went home to our Rutherford Table mining camp determined to return as soon as possible to Mackay to attend a healing meeting at the church.

A few days later as I loaded dirt into our truck to be taken to the washing plant, I asked God if it was possible for me to praise Him too much because I wanted to speak in other tongues again. This prompted me to get down on my knees to speak in my new prayer language. Quite a while later, refreshed and peaceful, I got up from this experience of praising God. By this time, Ada was concerned because I was half-an-hour overdue. Usually, I did two trips an hour to and from the plant which she supervised.

Several weeks later, we rose very early, as we were finally going to New-Way Church in Mackay to attend our first-ever healing meeting there. It was a five-hour trip and, as was our habit, we'd prepared well with spare wheels, fuel, tools and spare parts, as the gravel roads were treacherous in places. Greg remained at camp to continue mining operations as he didn't really understand what had happened to us in Brisbane. Ada and I were excited, full of anticipation at what God might do for us as we were believing Him for physical healing. We drove sixty-five kilometres south through Mt Coolon, and then a further 105 kilometres of the same dirt, dust and gullies before we reached the bitumen road to Mackay.

We entered the church right on time not knowing what to expect and were struck by the love and happiness of the people who had gathered there. They were so friendly and shook our hands as if they'd known us for ages. The massive sign behind the pulpit, 'JESUS IS LORD' impressed us as the right place to receive healing. Like parched travellers, we drank in the words of the preacher as he told of the miracle, life-changing power of Jesus Christ. Faith rose in our hearts and, when he invited those who needed healing to come forward for prayer, I was one of the first in the healing line.

My most pressing need was my right shoulder. I'd worked hard physically all my life and the years had taken their toll on my body. My right arm had begun to lose its strength several months previously. Arthritis had set in, causing severe pain in the shoulder. It limited the use of my arm, sapping it of nearly all its natural strength. My shoulder had become so painful that I couldn't lift my arm to comb my hair. I struggled with much of the heavy mining work and being naturally right-handed, I taught myself to use my left arm for many jobs. I had even trained myself to comb my hair with my left hand.

The pastor came to me and prayed that I be healed in the Name of Jesus. Then he took my right arm, stretched it straight out in front of me then quickly raised it straight above my head. I felt three distinct cracks in my right shoulder but no pain whatsoever. My arm was perfectly healed in an instant, while at the same time "Praise the Lord" came out of my mouth for the first time ever in my life; and in public, too! This was an amazing introduction into what can happen when you live your life 'in Jesus'.

I also had a stomach ulcer that had debilitated me for a long time. I had learned to live with it by using herbal medicines. Even though I wanted it healed that day, I thought I couldn't ask God for too much at one time. I've learned a lot since then – He's a limitless God! The pastor continued to pray for others in the healing line guided by the anointing of Holy Spirit. Ada was overcome by the anointing and presence of Holy Spirit even before the pastor reached her, however, God had shown him that she needed more prayer. After some time, she got up from the floor and he returned to minister to her. When she said, "I feel as if I haven't got my money's worth yet" he replied, "What do you mean, I haven't taken up the offering yet." The congregation broke into laughter. God is good and He delights to bless His people in every way, including healing.

After the service, the pastor informed the congregation that we had driven close to five hours to attend the meeting, and asked if anyone would offer to take us home for lunch. A lovely couple were happy to do so, and that was the beginning of a wonderful and deep friendship of over forty years until they both left us to go to their heavenly home with the Lord. Later, we went to the weekday healing meetings also.

After the miracle of our salvation, the healing miracles we received that Sunday were the beginning of God's amazing interventions in our family life. During the weeks that followed, Greg couldn't help but notice the changes that had occurred in both Ada and me.

Chapter 7

Greg's story: "In January 1981 when I was holidaying at a friend's place in Townsville, Dad rang while they were on their way home from Sydney. We arranged to meet at Bowen so that we could travel back to our Rutherford Table camp together. Dad said during the call that we've got a lot to talk about when we get home. I could tell immediately that there was something different about him. I knew it was more than just news about Nan or the other relatives. When they returned home, I certainly noticed changes in Mum and Dad, mainly Dad.

In our mining work, Dad and I were having physical difficulties because there were things that I couldn't lift because of my back, and other things Dad couldn't lift because of his shoulder which had

Greg Miers

deteriorated to the point where he couldn't lift his arm even to comb his hair. My back troubles were caused by slipped discs which hindered my work sometimes for weeks. The chiropractor could get my back into working order, but it wouldn't stay that way.

Sometime after their return, they went to a Thursday morning healing meeting in Mackay, where Dad's shoulder was completely healed. After that, he could lift anything! This really impressed me because I needed healing, too. Dad had received an obvious miracle and I was absolutely fascinated to hear of what had happened, but most of all I wanted to see something like that for myself.

I had worked in opal and sapphire mines in western Queensland for several years, underground mainly, in shafts and small caverns. As a result of working in the confined spaces, hunched over and carrying heavy weights, my back had begun to give out. Several slipped discs slowed me down, causing great discomfort and pain during much of my working time. I learned to squat when I picked up things off the ground, not bend; or I would bend over sideways, but never forward. Only those who have had a spinal injury know the pain it can cause as you try to work. All my visits to the doctors and chiropractors had no lasting effect and the injury became steadily worse.

I couldn't quite understand what had happened to my parents, so I decided to have a look for myself. I thought, *I need a piece of this action* and a couple of months later I decided to visit the church to get healed. As I drove towards Mackay, I thought, *If I can see it, I will believe it, if only I can see it.* I wasn't looking to be saved because I didn't know that had happened to them.

I didn't want to go into the church on my own, so I asked an old bloke with whom we had business dealings, and whom we knew was in a bad way, to come with me to the Thursday healing meeting. He couldn't do anything much, as he was always short of breath with an undiagnosed condition. He had a lot of other problems too, including a severe kidney disorder. At the meeting we both listened intently as the preacher explained the good news of Jesus Christ. Our faith began to build as it was made clear that 'Jesus is the same yesterday, today, and forever' and is still in the miracle-working business. Not quite sure what to expect, both of us accepted an invitation for prayer and walked to the end of the prayer line. My business acquaintance was the first to be touched by the power of God as he stood there. Completely overcome by God's power he collapsed to the floor, tears streaming down his face as the pain in his kidneys miraculously disappeared. Several days later he passed a stone. Jesus the Healer had touched his body even before the pastor had laid his hands on anyone or prayed for anybody. The Holy Spirit was present to heal and to save.

Soon after this, the pastor came down from the platform and asked the nature of my problem. While explaining about my back, I was amazed to find myself falling to the floor as the pastor prayed for the healing power of God to touch every part of my spine, in Jesus' Name. When I was able to get up from the floor the pastor said, "Touch your toes", and I could. He then said, "Run up the stairs and back down", and I could. I had no pain! The whole congregation began to clap and praise God for this demonstration of His love and healing power. There was a solidly built young fellow standing nearby and the pastor called him over and ordered me to pick him up and carry him around the platform. Not a problem. No pain! My back was perfectly healed and restored in strength in a moment of time.

We had both gone out for prayer and both of us were totally healed. I had driven 320 kilometres to Mackay, expecting to get healed and that's what happened. There were no cracks or snaps like at the chiropractor; Jesus just fixed me. The pastor told me to bend down and pick up one of the musicians. I didn't really think about it, I just did what the pastor told me to do. I didn't feel any pain, I simply acted and was amazed. No pain!

Not long after this, in the same meeting, there was an altar call, so the old bloke and I went out and got saved, even though I didn't really understand what I was doing at the time. However, I was never the same again! I was learning what living 'in Jesus' is all about, just like Dad and Mum. There were others in the meeting who were saved, too. No one talked to us after the service, so I didn't really know what we'd done. After the service, the old bloke walked with me a full block down the street; something he hadn't done for many years. When I arrived home and explained that I'd been prayed for and had repeated a prayer, Mum said, "Oh, you got saved!" Dad then gave me a little bible to read which the Lutheran Church at Alberton had given to Shelley years before.

Two months later in May 1981, I went to Mackay again for a few days but ended up staying for ten. While I attended a convention on the first few days, the Spirit of God touched me and on Sunday afternoon, in obedience to the Word of God, I was water baptised by a youth leader from New-Way Outreach Ministries who prayed that I receive the baptism of the Holy Spirit. I didn't speak in tongues then, but I was so full of the joy of the Lord, I could hardly contain it. Being alive felt so good!

Later that evening in a public shower in the caravan park where I was staying, as I turned on the water the power of the Holy Spirit fell all over me again. My knees buckled and as I sank to the floor with the shower still running, I began to speak in other tongues. My new God-given language just flowed out uncontrollably.[21] I had received the promise of the Holy Spirit. It was like in the Book of Acts, chapter 2 all over again. I tried to keep the sound down, but the Lord had filled me to overflowing. After about fifteen minutes, I managed to stagger to my feet and peered sheepishly out the door to see who was listening. No one appeared to be there (I wonder why?) so I dressed hastily, skipped dinner, and rushed off

---

21 Actually, I could stop, I just didn't want to!

to the meeting. When you get so full of the Lord, meals don't seem to be that important. Arriving back home, it was Dad and Mum's turn to listen to what had happened during my time away. They couldn't keep me quiet for a week!"

Chapter 8

A few weeks later, in a mutual exchange of work for a neighbouring mining company, I (Des) was to build a new access road with our TD24 bulldozer. It was uncomfortably hot and dirty work as I maneuvered the 'dozer through the scrub. The jarring was incredible as the 'dozer jerked and twisted over the rough ground. The steel tracks regularly rode over a boulder then thumped the machine back onto level ground and trees broke and fell behind me. Vibrations constantly jolted me, badly upsetting my stomach ulcer to the point where I was finally forced to submit to the stabbing pain. I shut the motor down to get some relief and considered my situation. The ulcer had become a fact of life over the previous fourteen years. I had learned to live with it; using special milk and egg diets, ulcer medicine and so on, I could get by. However, the jolting and jerking of the massive 'dozer had caused the ulcer to flare up.

The pastor of New-Way Church understood that we, as new believers living remotely in the bush, needed good, solid teaching in the Word of God so that we could mature in our faith. Our attendance at the Mackay church was infrequent due to the distance, so he gave us teaching tapes by Derek Prince and David Pawson. We devoured them and learned how to take our Godly authority against the evil forces of darkness and became established in the knowledge of the scriptures.

We had listened to these cassettes repeatedly and learned how God could heal. I had no doubt it was God's will to heal me. I reasoned that if God could heal me in Mackay, couldn't He heal me here in the bush? I prayed right then and there, "Please, Lord. I'm in trouble and need your help." I didn't feel any obvious sign of being answered, but over the space of a few minutes, the pain went completely and my stomach felt good. As it was about 2pm, I restarted the 'dozer and went back to work for the remainder of the afternoon. When I got home that night, I told Ada what had happened and then rounded up all the ulcer medicines and threw them in the garbage bin, believing and acting like I was totally healed, which I actually was. I shouted, "I'll never need that stuff again. I am healed!" and I've never needed it since. Jesus completely healed the ulcer and removed all the pain, thus enabling me to eat anything I desire. Spices, garlic, cabbage, onions, coffee, tea and peas – previously, all forbidden foods – became part of my daily diet again. Prior to this I wouldn't go anywhere without my medicines; our family had been like a travelling chemist shop. Now I can eat anything, praise the Lord!

As our pastor saw the incredible things that God was doing in our lives, he wanted to know more which led him to ask if he could write our story. He brought his wife and children to stay for a week at our mining camp, during which time he asked lots of questions and observed the conditions of our remote locality. Subsequently, using the church's printing press he produced a book, *Miracles Beyond the Black Stump*, which details the miracles and healings we experienced during the first ten months of our Christian journey.[22]

Around that time, the local shire council planned to impose fees on miners' leases and during a meeting at a Collinsville motel with other

---
22 Some of the above miracle healing story is adapted from *Miracles Beyond the Black Stump* (out of print).

concerned miners, I met a new friend. Later, we achieved some success when the council reduced the miners' fees. Our new friend invited Ada and me to Bowen that night to share a meal and stay overnight at a beach house. As part of the meal, his wife served cabbage and peas, which, up until then, I hadn't eaten in ever so long due to its impact on my stomach ulcer. I cautiously accepted a stubby of beer and made it last the night as I hadn't had a beer in many years for the same reason. By daylight, I was awake with a thumping headache from that one beer and so I asked the Lord to remove the pain. Instantly, the pain left, and I couldn't wait to wake Ada to tell her about another miracle!

During that evening, I told my new friends of the miracles that the Lord had done for Ada and me. The husband said later that he needed healing, as two-thirds of one of his lungs had been surgically removed and there were spots on the other lung. He was a farmer experiencing difficulty in doing his work, including climbing the steps to his high-set Queenslander house. He asked lots of questions, so we told him about the church at Mackay. He asked to accompany us the next time we planned to attend.

A few weeks later we called to let him know that we were going to Mackay for an evening service. He flew his light plane into Mackay and we met him at the airport. He said later that he'd nearly turned around halfway; going to church was something that he never did! His wife and he had different views about the church – he was happy for her to attend, providing she never wanted him to do so. We spent the afternoon together sharing about our God experiences; the healings and miracles He had done for us.

That night I walked with him when the pastor called for anyone who wanted prayer. There was a line of people who had responded to the invitation and the pastor moved up and down the line. He prayed for some, and just lightly touched others on the head. My friend was one of those. When that happened, his knees buckled and he slumped to the floor under the power of God. He picked himself up, flabbergasted. He was a man who could handle himself and he knew how to floor someone if the need arose. The pastor continued to walk up and down the line and touched him again on the head. Again, he hit the floor, unable to stand under God's power. He struggled to his feet, overwhelmed that no one other than God could have done what had just happened to him. God firmly had his attention at this stage! Eventually, the pastor prayed for his healing and my friend decided that he wanted God in his life. In other words, he was saved.[23]

As soon as the service ended, he couldn't find a phone box fast enough – this was before the advent of mobile phones – to tell his wife what he had done. He really discovered God's goodness when, at his quarterly medical check-up and x-rays, the doctor told him that the lung that had been surgically reduced to one third was now whole and complete, and there were no longer spots on his other lung! His wife later had her own conversion to Jesus Christ.

---

23 Acts 16:31. So they said, "Believe on the Lord Jesus Christ, and you will be saved, you and your household."

Chapter 9

Greg had received a prophecy that he would leave our mining operation to serve the Lord. Subsequently, the church helped fund him to be part of a YWAM[24] outreach team at the Los Angeles Olympic Games in 1984. Greg's departure was difficult for us, as it meant we would lose his help, so I whinged to the Lord about the situation. "You've taken my son and I know Your needs are greater than mine, but I need some help so can You replace him?" The following morning, just before I started the washing plant, the Lord spoke very clearly, "What you need is a sixteen-year-old boy." My response was an incredulous, "What use would he be to me?" I didn't receive a reply.

That same afternoon, a former caretaker of a nearby mining property and his son visited us. When I saw the lad get out of the car I said to the Lord, "You have to be kidding – not him!" I knew this boy a few years prior and he had been

---
24 Youth with a Mission.

a real nuisance. It seemed that he was always in trouble. After the usual greetings, I asked him his age and of course, he said sixteen. I said under my breath, "Lord, you have to be joking!" I didn't want to touch him with a barge pole. As the conversation continued, I asked the lad what he was doing with himself; he was looking for a job! Apprehensive at the prospect of having this fellow on our property, after a cup of tea[25] I realised that it must be God's will to have him work for us. I relented and offered him a temporary job, as I didn't want to commit too deeply. His father said that he would pick up his son two or three weeks later. Well, to my surprise, that boy was a real blessing to us; he did whatever was asked of him and he did it well. God knew we needed him and we had many opportunities to tell our God stories and to sow the Word of God. When the time came for him to finish up, we were sorry to see him leave.

As new believers, we usually attended church in Bowen, as it was only half the distance that Mackay was from our camp. We planned

---

25 There is no problem on earth that can't be ameliorated by a hot bath and a cup of tea – Jasper Fforde.

church attendance to coincide with trips to town for supplies about every eight weeks. At morning church one Sunday in December, Jenny Smith, whom we didn't know, gave us a Christmas card. When we went back to church that night, the pastor mentioned that Brian and Jenny, a young couple who were new in the church, didn't have anyone with whom to spend Christmas. Prior to this, we had made Christmas arrangements to visit Greg, who lived with three guys in a halfway house owned by his church in Mackay, so we invited the Smiths to Greg's place. We didn't know then that Brian had been out of work and had to borrow the money to be able to drive to Mackay. That was the beginning of our connection to the Smith family.

We didn't have any contact with them for a while, until about midnight one night, Brian called. The family were near Marlborough, on their way to Brisbane to see Jenny's mum, when their car went over an embankment. It was very heavy grass where they had landed and none of them were hurt, sustaining only scratches. However, Brian needed help to get his smashed car and family home.

I didn't get much sleep that night. Before I could hook up our trailer, I had to build ramps so we could get his car up onto the trailer. After a five-hour drive to Marlborough, I located them, loaded their car and drove them back to their home in Bowen. I then drove another two hours to get home to Rutherford Table. After that experience, Brian looked to us as his dad and mum because he'd never known anyone to help him the way that we had. Over the years, the Smiths became as close or closer to us than most of the people in our natural family. We stayed with them often when we were in Bowen. The Lord says that He sets the solitary in families.[26] The Smiths adopted us, and we adopted them. For a time, as he needed work, Brian used to come to Rutherford Table to help while I was building a mining machine.[27] This was another way that God blessed us with help after Greg left to get involved in mission work.

---

26 Psalm 68:6.
27 Greg, Brian and I built a mining machine, which was a scaled-down version I'd designed after seeing one at the Collinsville coal mine. My version had a truck engine and worked as an underground digger. It had hydraulic pumps and rams, blowers (big fans) – the front blade moved up and down; other blades moved the dirt through a hole onto a conveyor belt that took it through to the back, from where it went into a hopper. Two hundred millimetre lay-flat piping took the dirt back to a place where we could cart it out. It carried the diesel exhaust out of the mine as well. One hydraulic pump drove a high-speed motor for the flat fan. There were extendable arms for the cutting head; one for the cutting head itself; conveyor belt; and six or seven hydraulic pumps that could operate independently or together.

Miracles In The Aussie Bush

The underground mining machine
that Des, Greg and Brian built.

During this time Ada and I drove to Ayr to buy parts for the next stage in building the mining machine. On arrival, we checked into our overnight accommodation and bought a can of boysenberries and a packet of liverwurst from the supermarket to add to our lunch. By late afternoon both of us had upset stomachs. Returning to our motel, I opened the back of our Landcruiser and removed our suitcases. I went inside and, feeling quite ill, collapsed on the bed alongside Ada. During the night I woke, startled. I saw in a vision a huge being – perhaps an angel? – standing with his hand on the roof of our vehicle. I thought immediately about the gold and sapphires that were in the car[28] as I had forgotten to lock the 'cruiser that afternoon. Was he protecting our vehicle, or reassuring me that all was well? He probably did both. I got up and checked the car, but there wasn't anyone around nor anything untoward. By the way, it was a long time before we ate liverwurst again.

Ada had suffered with severe migraine headaches for many years. The pain was so severe that any form of light, loud noise or bumps would cause intense suffering. Sometimes the headache would be unbearable, forcing her to bed for three days at a time. On long car trips, she would wear dark glasses to cover her eyes, prop a pillow under her head and hope not to get a migraine.

In the early days of our new-found faith, we traveled to Mackay about every month and our first port of call was always the church. One day Ada waited patiently for the healing line to begin. She had received prayer for the migraines previously and had received partial relief. By this stage in our Christian experience, she knew

---

[28] Worth about $4,000; too valuable to leave unattended at home.

that God could heal her. She asked the pastor for prayer again for the migraine and for her back. Though her back wasn't as bad as Greg's, it had troubled her for twenty-three years, limiting movement and causing sharp pain from time to time. She had slept on boards and tried everything. As the pastor put one hand on Ada's forehead and one on her spine he prayed for healing in the Name of Jesus. At that moment, the power of God flowed from her head right down her spine. She fell to the floor, unable to stand under His power. The pastor prayed for others on the line for about ten minutes and then he came back to her exclaiming to others, "I hope she wakes up soon. I want to see her back healed". Jesus, the Master Physician, healed her spine. When He had finished, she came up off the floor with a jump knowing she was healed! She threw her arms around the pastor and shouted, "Praise the Lord!" for the first time ever in public. The congregation burst into praising the Lord. From that time Ada hasn't had back trouble or migraines. No more pain, no more pills.

One Sunday at church, the pastor called Ada and me forward for prayer because we were to return to our camp the next day, back to its isolation and lack of Christian fellowship. We stood together, arms around each other, before the congregation. He prayed, "Father, in the Name of Jesus, keep them as they travel and let your Spirit be upon them." Immediately, we were slain in the Spirit,[29] triggering another series of miracles in our lives.

Ada had suffered with poor circulation in her right arm for many years which caused great discomfort if she happened to sleep on it. Next morning she woke lying on her right arm. *Oh no!* she thought. As usual, she rolled over and hung her arm over the side of the bed, allowing it to dangle until the circulation was restored, the pins and needles feeling gone and strength returned. However, this time something was different. There was no sensation of pins and needles. No numbness. Her hand moved perfectly normally. Jesus had healed the problem without her asking. "Praise the Lord!" she exclaimed. Being healed and praising the Lord was becoming quite a habit.

---

29 'Slain in the Spirit' is a term used in Charismatic and Pentecostal circles to describe what happens when the Spirit of God comes upon a person and they are physically unable to stand.

Several weeks later, Ada was going about her ordinary, everyday chores when she noticed suddenly that her hands were different. The skin on her hands had been cracked and scaled, plagued by dermatitis since she had worked in the sapphire mines years before. Embarrassed by the obvious condition of her hands, she would use a nail file to smooth the skin before each trip to town, but now they were different. The skin was clear without a trace of dermatitis. Another miracle!

Greg also had a miracle concerning an allergy. Every few weeks he reacted to an unknown irritant, perhaps dust or pollen, which caused itchy lumps to appear all over his body. Doctors had prescribed pills to relieve the problem but were unable to cure it. When Greg heard about the healing to Ada's hands, he realised that he hadn't been troubled by the allergy for over three months. Another miracle!

Several times I had benign polyps grow on the inside of my throat. Surgery was necessary to remove them, followed by a painful period of recovery and medication. Shortly after the Lord healed my ulcer, I noticed that another polyp had formed in the back of my throat. It continued to grow until it was quite large and I felt something had to be done about it. What would I do? Go to the doctor or pray? I prayed, "Please Lord, take away this thing. Whatever is wrong, please make it like new." The polyp began to diminish in size until it finally disappeared and has not returned since.

All the foregoing miracles in our family took place over a period of ten months after we gave our lives to Jesus Christ. Not long after we were born again, one of the counsellors at the Mackay church said to Ada after a healing meeting, "You will want to eat, sleep and drink Christianity; you will enjoy it so much." Ada thought that was incredulous, yet, we have done just that! God became part of our daily lives. Way out back of beyond in the loneliness of the Australian bush, the Lord Jesus Christ proved to be a reality for us three. Whenever anything went wrong, we'd stop, lay hands on each other, pray, and God gave us miracles.

Des, Ada, Greg and Shelley in Mackay

Twelve months after we became Christians, our daughter Shelley came to holiday with us at Mackay, and in early January 1982 she too, accepted Jesus Christ as her Saviour and was baptised in the pastor's swimming pool the following day. We played the tourist and picnicked at Eungella National Park, near Mackay. We had eaten watermelon while standing at the back of the Land Cruiser with the tailboard down for a table. When we'd finished, Ada and Shelley went to the rest rooms and I cleaned and packed away. As I walked around the side of the vehicle, I felt there was a needle sticking in my big toe. I reached down and saw that I'd been bitten by a red jumper ant.[30] They are aggressive and search you out if you get near their territory. I was allergic to these ants, as I had been bitten many times when I was a child. My throat would swell and get very itchy, so I ensured that there were always antihistamine tablets in the glove box of the car. As I reached for the catch on the glove compartment, I heard, *you don't need that*. I immediately remembered the scripture, "... and if they drink anything deadly, it will by no means hurt them ..."[31] So, I sat back, prayed, and asked God for His help.[32] When Ada and Shelley returned I told them what had happened. I was amazed that my foot didn't swell, nor my throat itch. We spent the rest of the day walking and enjoying the Park and I had no ill effects.

---

30 This red jumper ant was probably of the family Myrmecia pilosula, a species of venomous ant native to Australia.
31 Mark 16:17-18: (Jesus speaking) "And these signs will follow those who believe: in My name they will cast out demons; they will speak with new tongues; they will take up serpents; and if they drink anything deadly, it will by no means hurt them; they will lay hands on the sick, and they will recover."
32 At this stage in our Christian development, we hadn't learned to take our authority as believers to command healing in Jesus Name. That came later.

A year later we were in Sydney again to see Nan, and I discovered a lump about the size of a 20-cent piece just below my right rib. On our way back to Rutherford Table we passed through Brisbane and visited Mansfield Christian Outreach Centre where Pastor Clark Taylor was preaching. At one stage, he stopped and said, "Someone has just found a lump under their right rib. Come out because God wants to heal you." I waited a moment or two for someone else to claim his word about it, but it was for me! I went forward and he prayed for me. The lump didn't disappear immediately, however, a few days later I noticed it was gone, and I've never had a problem with it since.

Chapter 10

One evening, strangers drove around our washing plant after dark. We were suspicious because the day's washed gold was still in the race, ready for collection the next morning. We took a rifle and put some lead into the hills above the car and scared them off. Sometime later, friends on their way to visit us got lost and ended up at a neighbour's place asking for directions. The neighbour said they shouldn't visit us after dark, because "those people shoot first and ask questions later."

We planned a break away for a couple of days, but I was concerned about an unsavoury looking group of people who were camped very close to the road where we were to pass. I had some valuable equipment and supplies scattered around our camp that would be easy pickings for anyone who had a mind to help themselves. To give the impression that one of us was still at camp, when we left I wore Ada's wig while she lay down on the seat as we passed by the group of itinerants.

A few days after we returned home, a friend phoned, as he was planning to visit. He mentioned that he'd called us some days earlier and had been told that we were away and would be back in two days. I hesitated, trying to make sense of what he'd said, and asked him who had told him we were away. He didn't know, except 'they' had told him. I didn't know what to make of this, so continued with the conversation.

When he arrived, I asked him again what had happened during that call when 'they' told him we would be back in two days. However, he couldn't add anything further to satisfy my curiosity. What I do know is that when we returned to our camp, everything was untouched and in order and our living quarters, where the landline phone was installed, was still securely locked. No one had been in there, so who had answered my friend's call? I can only guess that it had been an angel. Whoever it was, we believe it was further evidence of God's goodness and protection over us.

We wanted to buy another vehicle and found a white HT Holden sedan[33] with a sticker in the rear window that said, 'Find buried treasure, read your Bible.' It was an easy decision; as gold miners and Christians, we knew this was the one!

One day in Mackay we had a picnic at the Botanic Gardens. While enjoying our lunch, we noticed a young couple walk along the track behind our car, cuddle, walk on and around us in a large circle, pausing along the way. That evening at the caravan park where we were staying, pain developed in my chest. Thinking I should go to the hospital, I talked myself out of doing so, as I reasoned that our tight financial position didn't allow for Ada to stay in rented accommodation if there was something seriously wrong with me. I sat up most of the night, suffering with the pain.

At daybreak, while I was in the bathroom, I heard the Lord say, "There is a strong satanic influence in this town. Pray against it." Immediately, I had a vision of the young couple who had circled us in the park, and then knew why the heart pain had occurred. It seemed that they had spoken a curse over me,

---

33 Holden Australia produced the HT Holden sedan in 1969-1970.

so I promptly prayed against it and exercised my Christian authority against the attack, just as we had learned to do from Derek Prince's[34] teaching tapes. The pain lifted within a few minutes and we went about our business for the day. We learned later from a friend of Greg's who worked at Mackay Hospital, that there was a witches' coven established there. I praise God that I didn't go to the hospital!

Living in the bush we often noticed wild European bees. In daylight we'd cut down the trees where the hives were and return after dark with a smoker, as they were less ferocious then, to clean out the honey. Ada made our protective head coverings from cardboard boxes with a full-face flyscreen gauze insert, and we wore white overalls and white gloves. One night, tired and sticky, we'd almost finished robbing a hive when a station wagon came along the narrow bush track where we had parked our vehicle. It was the old miner and a couple of his mates well primed from the pub,

---

[34] Derek Prince was an international Bible teacher, author, pastor, missionary and theologian. He was born 1915 in Bangalore, India of British parents and died 2003 (aged 88) in Jerusalem, Israel.

with a 200 litre drum of fuel in the back and, as he couldn't get around our car, had to stop.

To move our car, I had to walk out of the bush wearing this weird white outfit. The next day, the old miner said that when he saw us loom out of the dark that he was close to having a heart attack! We felled six trees for honey in the time we were at Rutherford Table and I still have some of it, over thirty years later, because pure honey doesn't deteriorate.

We mined gold at Rutherford Table for about twelve years. We lived and worked in hot, dry, barren, Brahman cattle country, with no air conditioning, even when the temperature was forty-five degrees Centigrade, and no rain for nine months at a time. Amid this, Ada grew a great vegetable garden and fruit trees using water and soil from the creek about a kilometre away. Our friend who owned a plane used to say that, from the air, our camp looked like an oasis in the desert.

Over my long years of mining, working in rough and tough conditions, I fell several times onto my back. On one occasion, I fell off an oil drum onto rocks; another time, I fell between steel benches, and while forcing an old, forged metal crowbar, it snapped and hit me in the head with such force that I fell backwards. To the best of my memory, I got up off the ground and went back to work, free of injury every time. I praise God for His protection!

Ada and Des with an abundant harvest at Rutherford Table

One morning I prepared for a trip to Mt Coolon to refuel our tanker and fuel drums. I loaded the tanker and drums onto the 1971 Albion Reiver truck and told Ada that if I wasn't home by late afternoon that she should start looking for me.[35] In hindsight, I have no idea why I said, "by late afternoon."

Around midday, refueled and about fifteen kilometres from camp the truck began to slow, even though I pushed hard on the accelerator. As it coasted to a stop, I steered to position myself under a shady tree off the road. Racking my brain as to why the vehicle was powerless, I talked to the Lord about my dilemma. Ada would not come looking for me until evening, which meant a four- to five-hour wait, and when she did arrive, she would be driving the Landcruiser. We would then return to camp and drive the Huff front-end loader back to the truck and tow it home. This presented another problem: there wasn't a second seat on the loader for Ada to travel with me to the truck, so she would need to drive the 'cruiser back to the truck. Yet another problem ... she had never driven the truck, nor towed it of course, nor had she ever driven the loader. Could she drive one of them? And how then would we get the 'cruiser

---

[35] Mt Coolon is a 130 kilometre round trip, which took about three hours, including the refuelling.

back home? We couldn't leave the truck overnight in this isolated spot, as it was likely that the fuel would be stolen. My head spun, trying to work it all out.

As I continued to tell the Lord about all my problems, I asked if He could get me home. He spoke very clearly, saying that I should "Put it [the truck] in diff-lock." I replied, "It doesn't work."[36] He spoke again, a little more strongly, "Put it in diff-lock." I replied again, "It does not work." He spoke a third time, more forcefully, "Put it in diff-lock." It was only then that I realised I was having an argument with the Lord!

I climbed back in the truck, started the engine, put it in gear and diff-lock and cautiously drove away. I went from gear to gear, praying in other tongues. And more so, as I encountered the single-lane bridge with the steep incline on the other side. The air brakes weren't brilliant, and I was concerned about stalling on the incline. That would have been a disaster. But the old truck kept going and got me home. I parked right at home base and went inside to tell Ada what had happened. There was rejoicing in the camp and much praise to God for getting me home.

---

36 When we purchased the truck some years before, we discovered that the diff-lock didn't work. We dismantled it for repairs but couldn't buy the necessary part to do the job. We didn't think about it any further and drove the vehicle knowing that the diff-lock didn't work.

After lunch I went to drive the truck to the overhead fuel tank to pump out the fuel drums and found that the truck wouldn't move. I then realised that I had asked the Lord to get me home and that is what happened. I had not asked to drive around the camp when I got there! Later I found that the splines on the tail shaft had been worn away over time. It was a miracle that got me home. All glory to God for what He did for us. When I replaced the tail shaft, I was able to drive the truck, but the diff-lock never worked again.

Des's truck – an Albion Reiver[37]

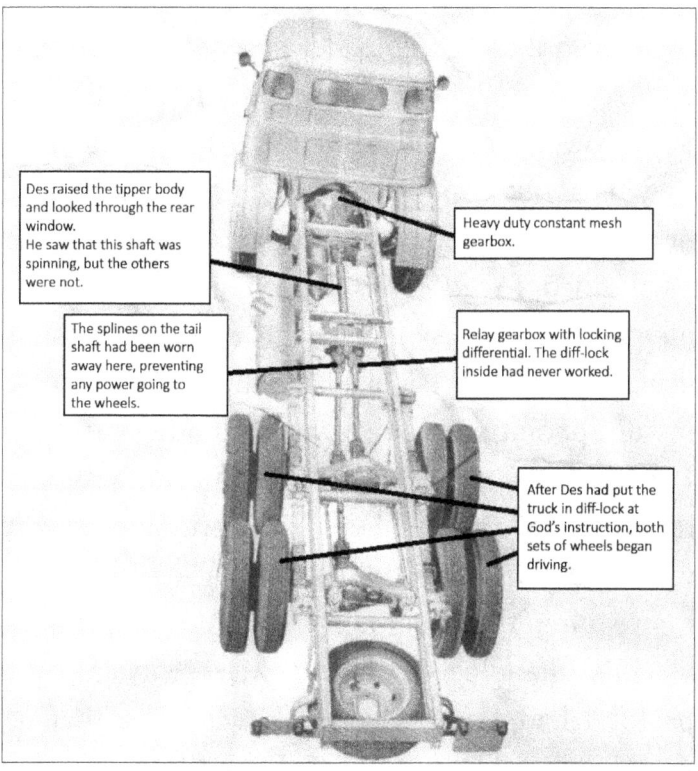

---

37 The relay gearbox splits the drive to the two rear axles and an inter-axle differential is incorporated in the box, and this is provided with a lock for use under off-road or similar adverse conditions. The lock for the differential is brought into action by air pressure controlled from the cab. If one tail-shaft stopped working, then the other one would not work either, unless the diff-lock was engaged. Source: 'Double-drive Albion Reivers', https://archive.commercial-motor.com/article/10thnovember-1961/100/the-super-reiver

On another occasion, I had to change a front-end loader wheel that was about two thirds my height, about the size of a grader wheel. After I removed it from the loader and onto the ground and repaired it, I struggled to lift it back on. Somehow, I managed, although I don't remember praying about it, but the exertion caused a rupture in my groin. I hobbled around for days afterwards so decided to go to a Sunday evening healing meeting in Townsville, which was a four hour drive. On arrival, I looked for the pastor who, to my disappointment, was away at another meeting. I said to the Lord, "We've come all this way and the pastor isn't even here." The worship leader, whose hair was in dreadlocks, was also responsible for leading the meeting. I was not impressed, as this dreadlocked fellow was replacing the pastor I had come to see. After deciding that he wouldn't be able to fulfill my expectations, I felt the conviction of Holy Spirit and repented.[38] During the worship time, the leader stopped abruptly and announced that someone had a bad pain in the lower part of their body and that God wanted to heal it. Having already repented of my judgmental attitude, I went forward and received

---

[38] To turn away from an ungodly attitude and to ask the Lord for forgiveness.

the prayers that he offered. By the next morning the pain had gone and I was healed. Scripture says, "Judge not, that you be not judged."[39]

Another time, while visiting Mackay on business, Ada decided to get her hair permed. However, after being tested by the hairdresser, she was told that her hair would not hold a perm. Ada shared her disappointment with the lovely couple who hosted us, and the wife said we could pray about it, which we did. The next day, Ada went back to the hairdresser and requested another test. Initially, the hairdresser was reluctant, knowing the previous day's result, but Ada insisted, and to the hairdresser's amazement Ada's hair had changed and so she got her lovely head of curls. This showed us that God not only wants to provide for our needs but also our wants, too!

Ada had been to see the doctor about change of life symptoms, hot flushes and so forth

---

[39] Matthew 7:1

and was prescribed several medications. Not happy about taking them, a wonderful Christian friend prayed for her, with the result that she didn't need to take any of the prescriptions and sailed through that time without any of the associated problems of menopause.

As we were hungry to grow spiritually, we subscribed to a Christian audio tape ministry and received ten teaching messages each month. This was years before the availability of the internet. Sometimes I duplicated some, as we thought they might be appreciated by Ada's mum in Sydney. Nan had never learned to read and thus wasn't able to read the Bible for herself, so the tapes helped her to grow spiritually, too. Over time though, she let these teachings slip by the wayside, probably because she didn't have Christian support around her. She became ill and was admitted to hospital. With that news, Ada and I went to Sydney and, with one of Ada's sisters, we found her unconscious, with lots of tubes monitoring her condition. It was impossible not to see a huge lump in the midsection of her body.

Following biblical instruction, Ada and I laid our hands on her and prayed that she be healed.[40] After a few minutes of prayer, suddenly Nan regained consciousness, flung her arms out wide and loudly exclaimed, "It's gone, it's gone, it's gone!" We didn't see the lump disappear, but the looseness of her hospital gown showed that the lump had indeed gone. Ada's sister, who had an asthma attack at the very same time, received the overflow of God's goodness and was healed too. The next day Nan sat in a chair and was discharged the day after!

---

40 Mark 16:18

Chapter 11

One time at the Rutherford Table camp, I filled the Landcruiser tank with petrol, intending to go somewhere, however, changed my mind. The next day, I dashed off to Bowen (about a 320 kilometre return trip) to buy some engine parts. A week later, after an equipment breakdown, I needed to go to Mackay, 300 kilometres away, for more parts. I rose before daybreak, and not remembering about the trip I'd made to Bowen, I assumed that I had a full tank and didn't even think about checking the fuel gauge. About 150 kilometres from camp, halfway between Mt Coolon and Nebo, I noticed the fuel gauge was on empty! We'd owned that vehicle for several years so I knew that when the gauge showed empty, it was empty. There was no fifty-kilometre reserve in the tank, like we have today.

I didn't know what to do ... it wasn't yet daylight and the day was going to be stinking hot. I couldn't contact camp as there were no mobile phones in those days. Should I head back to Mt

Coolon where there would be petrol, though I would have to wait hours for the service station to open? Maybe sit tight and hope that another car would come by? I knew that very little traffic used that road. Or should I try for Nebo where there would be fuel available?

As I considered my options I remembered a teaching tape by Kenneth Copeland, who experienced something similar. While flying across remote country during a storm he used all his plane's fuel when blown off course. When a plane's fuel gauge shows empty, it is empty. There is no reserve. Kenneth asked the Lord for His help, and then flew the plane for some time to his destination – I can't remember how many hours – on an empty tank. So, I reminded the Lord about what He had done for Kenneth. And then, I asked the Lord if He would get me out of trouble and get me to Nebo. Praying in other tongues, I headed to Nebo and arrived, still praying, having driven about 85 kilometres on an empty tank!

Another time, while doing business in Mackay we visited Greg's place and met a young chap who looked very fit and able. As we talked, I realised that he could be a potential worker for us, so I offered him a job. On the way together to our camp I noticed a few times that he seemed to be having a joke with himself and chuckling which I thought was a bit odd. Later, some of the other guys I employed said there was something not quite right with that fella.

He told me he could do building work, so I gave him instructions for extending an existing hip roof which provided shelter over our caravan. He had to dig four large postholes and plant three-inch pipes into them. The pipes had to be cut off at the right height to meet the adjoining roof line. When I returned later in the day, after having worked on repairs to the bulldozer, I was dumbfounded to see that the pipes had not been cut off, but instead were heading skywards at an angle that would never match up with the rest of the roof. I told him that he must have misunderstood me because what he'd done wasn't what I wanted. Without a word, he started swinging punches at me and I couldn't do anything because I was loaded with the 'dozer's self-starter under one arm and spanners in the other hand. I dropped my stuff and started trying to dodge the punches, but he caught me with a blow to the right side of my head. About this time, he started yelling, "I'll kill you, I'll kill you, I'll kill you!"

When Ada heard the commotion, she came around the side of the caravan and yelled, "You can't touch him, he's covered by the blood of Jesus!" He then stopped swinging at me and started towards her. Now I was mad! Right in front of me was a round-mouthed shovel, I grabbed it, brought it up over my head and yelled at him, "If you touch her, I'll split you straight down the middle!" At this, he turned around and came back at me. Fortunately, I didn't use the shovel on its edge, but with all my strength brought it down on his head, which should have dropped him. However, he just stood there with his eyes rolling a few times. He didn't move. I thought, *I've fired my best shot, what do I do now?* He continued to just stand there, looking at me; I don't know if it was for seconds or minutes! Then, with all the violence gone out of him, he said, "You've done a good job, you've done a good job." I didn't know what he meant, but I said, "And you've done yours. Hit the road, Jack."

God is always on time! It was around 3pm when this happened and out of the blue our friend and his wife in their light plane buzzed around our camp which was a signal that they were about to land and wanted me to pick them up from the airstrip about a kilometre away. They had never arrived late in the day, always in the morning. I didn't know what to do, as I couldn't take Ada with me and leave the maniac on his own at the camp. So, I gave Ada a loaded rifle, told her to go inside and lock the door and if he tried to come through for her, to fire through the door at him.

I went to meet the plane and told our friends of the predicament. The husband suggested he put the fellow in the plane and fly him to Collinsville, but his wife was adamant, "No way! You are not taking him up in the plane!" On the way back to camp, I suggested that he and I drive the fellow to Collinsville, seventy kilometres away, as I didn't want him anywhere near us. He would be able to find his own way if we took him there. It was storming over Collinsville when we arrived. Later, we learned that his mother had brought him from Rubyvale to the Mackay church, so he could be prayed for and delivered from a violent temper.

I thought that was the end of the story. Two-and-a-half years later in June, I received a letter addressed to *Dess, the goldminer, Collinsville*. He began with something unintelligible, but then, "You sure swing a mean shovel. Merry Christmas!" Clearly, I'd left a lasting impression on him! God's timing, intervention, and provision for us was obvious.

One day I was about to refuel our Huff front-end loader from 200-litre drums stored on our two-and-a-half-metre tandem trailer. Standing on one of the drums at the front of the trailer, I placed the fuel pump into one of them and started to step across the half-metre gap between the trailer to the loader, to open its fuel tank. In those days, I wore ex-Army lace-up boots with long boot laces, but as I began to move out over the gap, I realised I was standing on a loose boot lace and I couldn't move my feet. Falling towards the steel arms of the loader, the next thing I knew, I was two-and-a-half metres away from the loader, having been transported to the back of the trailer. This was impossible! In the natural realm there is no way I could have fallen in the opposite direction and travelled that distance. I didn't escape unscathed though, as I hit my tail bone on the trailer's tailboard when I landed on my feet at the back of the trailer, facing in the opposite direction from the loader. Ada saw me standing at the end of the trailer but did not actually see me being transported there. Scripture says, "For He shall give His angels charge over you, to keep you in all your ways. In their hands they shall bear you up, lest you dash your foot against a stone."[41]

It was about 4pm on the Nebo Road, eighty-six kilometres from Mackay where we'd been for business. We were on our way home in our faithful old Holden and with a loaded trailer. Straight ahead was a nasty looking storm. Very high winds blasted water into our engine and stalled our vehicle. Off the road, we considered our situation. We had learned from the Bible to speak to storms, just as Jesus had commanded, "Peace. Be still", and usually they dispersed without dropping any rain. Jesus also said, "... he who believes in me, the

---

[41] Psalm 91:11-12.

works that I do he will do also; and greater works than these he will do, because I go to my Father."[42] We then commanded the storm, "Peace, be still, in Jesus' Name." Within minutes, the violent winds stopped but the rain continued to bucket down. I found a can of WD40[43] and a covering for my head, dived out of the car, lifted the bonnet, sprayed the propellant on the distributor and got back into the car as fast as possible. I started the engine and we set off, very slowly because there was tree debris strewn across the road. Later that evening we found that we couldn't take our usual route home as roads were cut off by the deluge. The road to Mt Coolon was impassable and we couldn't return to Mackay because a small bridge had been washed out. Eventually, we returned via the coast road. Our total mileage for the trip was 950 kilometres, whereas usually it was about 600 kilometres. We arrived home exhausted the next morning, but ever so grateful to God for bringing us safely through.

---

42 John 14:12.
43 WD40 is a spray can propellant that disperses water, loosens nuts and bolts and penetrates rust.

One workday as I drove our fully loaded truck at low speed to the washing plant, the truck's steering rod broke which sent me off the road. The truck went through a large hole where I'd scooped out a bucketful of dirt with the front-end loader, and narrowly avoided a head-on crash with a substantial gum tree. The truck had been reinforced with seventy-five-millimetre metal bars on the sides of the tipper body, and as it scraped along the tree all the bars were bent backwards. Braking, I came to a halt without injury. Surely, I had experienced another one of God's interventions into our natural realm. Our experiences in the extreme conditions of the Aussie bush seemed to keep His angels busy!

Over the years, we had shared with relatives our stories about God's goodness to us and the healings and miracles we had witnessed and received. To my delight, my dearest aunty decided to accept and follow Jesus Christ as her Saviour. However, to the best of my knowledge, my Dad (her brother) never responded to any of the invitations I had offered him. One day we received a message that he had just died in Brisbane. Though I had worked most of the day, I prepared to drive overnight to Brisbane, about a 1,300-kilometre trip. Ada said she would pray for me to stay awake as I drove, and I said I would pray for her protection. At bedtime, Ada walked the fifty metres to the power generator to shut it off for the night. As she lay down, the whole wall of the caravan lit up. She was startled and afraid at first, thinking someone was shining a torch on the van and then realised that the light was inside, not outside. Then she just knew that it was the Lord's light, not anything natural and was immediately comforted, knowing His presence was there and so was His protection.

I arrived at Brisbane early the next morning, but too early to see my stepmother. I thought I'd wait out the time with a sleep; however, despite having worked most of the previous day and then driven all the way to Brisbane, I couldn't sleep. Once I returned home and talked with Ada, I realised the effectiveness of her prayers, for I had been kept awake all that long night.

Chapter 12

A friend had given Ada the recipe for a delightful ginger beer which was a very refreshing thirst quencher in our hot, dry climate. The recipe required sugar and powdered ginger to feed the 'plant' from which we made our brew. We did a shopping trip about every eight weeks because we were a long way out of town. One night as we were returning on a gravel road with a trailer load of shopping, I spotted what looked like a pair of reading glasses lying on the road. I stopped the vehicle, walked back with my torch, and was amazed to see two fifty-gram containers of powdered ginger standing upright in the middle of the road. Thinking it was a setup, I looked around to find a long stick and knocked one can over, then the other. They didn't explode! They were clean of dust and with unbroken seals, so I picked them up and returned to the car to show Ada. She was incredulous. She had forgotten to add ginger powder to her lengthy shopping list. We can only believe that God's angels had been busy again. It amazed us that Father God cared even about small things like an ingredient for our ginger beer.

Each October brought a lot of little storms and subsequent road washouts which stopped our work for several days. When the ground dried out we'd restore the roads with our heavy machinery. As mentioned earlier, following the example that Jesus gave us, we had learned to speak peace and stillness to storms and usually, no rain fell. The local grazier came by one time and said that he didn't understand the weather in recent times. While out working on his land he'd see storms brewing and head home expecting rain, but instead the clouds disappeared. Consequently, he wasn't getting any rain.

Storms while we were working the washing plant meant that we would have to shut it down. We had to clean out the gold every time we stopped the plant, otherwise the mats that lined the race that held the gold might dry out before the plant was restarted and water running again. If that happened, the water would flow across the top of the dry mats and pick up gold with it, and some would be carried away and lost in the slurry ponds. Storm interruptions meant we couldn't get that job done.

As that particular Christmas approached, we ran the plant for as many hours as possible to get enough finance together for a good holiday. We washed twenty-five cubic metres of gravel which was two truckloads, every hour. One day we could see four small storms across the expanse of sky, and so, as we usually did, spoke to them, commanding, "Peace. Be still" and asked the Lord to disperse the storms. I returned to the truck and headed to the area where I'd been loading gravel and ignored the clouds. But the rain came down in a deluge and with the road awash, I barely made it back to the plant which Ada had already shut down. I complained to the Lord about it, "If this is the way you treat your kids, I'm not impressed," and like spoilt brats we went back to camp and sulked all afternoon.

The next morning, knowing that we couldn't work the plant for a few days until the ground dried out, we pulled up the mats and cleaned them out. To our utter amazement the mats were sheets of yellow, an unbelievable amount of gold like we had never seen! I knew then what had happened the previous day; the quantity we had washed was way above our normal and there was too much gold for it to be held in the mats. We needed that storm so there was reason to shut down the plant, otherwise a lot of gold would have been washed away by the force of the plant's water flow and into the slurry ponds. It appeared that we had struck a patch of ground that the old Chinese miners had missed, and we had hit paydirt. That one morning's work before the storm was the equivalent to a week's worth of gold! I fell to my knees and asked God to forgive my complaining and faithless attitude.

Some of our experiences were quite disturbing. Jimmy, the caretaker at our old and unused mine asked if I could direct him to a spot in the mine where he might find some decent wash. I suggested a spot that we had never worked, as it might be worth looking at. We went there and, as I had a powder monkey's licence,[44] I set a couple of explosive charges. The blast

---

[44] An expression for someone who was licensed to use explosives, which I had done for many years.

loosened the gold bearing wash and achieved what we wanted. With that job done, we stopped for morning tea in an area of the tunnel known as 'the ballroom', which was about ten metres across and sat in the main drive amongst all our equipment. We then shovelled out the wash that had been loosened by the blast from a depression in the floor. At our lunch break we left our lights and equipment in the middle of the drive when we left the tunnel. Jimmy and I went our separate ways for lunch and on our return, we couldn't believe our eyes. A huge slab of 'slippery back'[45] from the roof, approximately three-quarters-of-a-metre thick had caved in, covered almost the full width of the drive and buried all the equipment, including a wheelbarrow, jack hammer and batteries. Jimmy recovered some of the wash and lost quite a bit of equipment.

Greg and I had noticed previously when working this mine with a little railway line inside the tunnel to the outside, that slabs would sheet off the wall and fall onto the line, always about midday. We don't know if this cave-in occurred a few minutes after we left for lunch or just before we returned, but if we'd been working there at the

---

45 A mixture of unstable sediment and light gravel, but mostly clay.

time it happened, I would not be telling this story. God had protected us, yet again!

Ada says of our mining years, "Wherever we lived, life was always hard work. At Rubyvale and Rutherford Table, add the heat and the dust! We just had to work and make do with what we had. But everything was different when we became Christians. Life seemed easier because we knew the Lord was with us. Before He was in our life, we used to work seven days a week but there was a big change once we realised the Lord's Day was meant for rest and time spent with Him. We held Sunday School in the afternoon for four little children of miners who lived down the road. They walked over to us all dressed up in their good clothes and we taught them from the Bible, followed with homemade cakes and drinks – maybe that's the reason they came. I don't know if they went on in relationship with the Lord, but we sowed into them what we could about the love of Jesus and His Word.

Those were the best years of our life! We had God's peace in our hearts, in the middle of nowhere. We saw God do so many wonderful things for us. We always had a testimony whenever we went to church on the coast, about some miracle or healing. It's because we had received so many miracles that our pastor wrote a book about what God had done for us.

One time, when Des and a neighbour, who lived about two kilometres away, were at odds over a land issue, his wife brought me a big box of vegetables and a bunch of sweet peas. She could not have known that I was low in food, especially vegetables and needing to feed two young Canadian men who had just arrived unexpectedly. But the Lord knew! Shelley had met them in Bible School in New South Wales and suggested they drop in on us while they were travelling around Queensland. Those two guys were great. They spent a few weeks with us and fenced my vegetable garden so vermin couldn't get in.

I started a little hobby of making greeting cards. Early on Sunday mornings I'd walk through the bush with a bucket of water so I could pick wildflowers. I'd press them and use the dried flowers to decorate the cards. I really enjoyed walking and talking to the Lord as I picked on those mornings. I'm sure He put flowers in my path so that I wouldn't miss them.

It seemed that I could grow everything. It must have been the weather, plenty of water from the creek and good soil. My paw-paws were beautiful and we took cases of them to Bowen to swap for tomatoes and other fruit and vegetables. I used to preserve my crops; beetroot and pickled cucumbers and pineapples which we bought in Bowen. We had chooks and pigeons for eggs and meat. Occasionally, one of the local graziers would bring over a side of beef in exchange for Des grading their roads. I'd then spend the morning cutting it up, salting and freezing it. The main groceries that we needed to buy were cereal ingredients and butter, margarine, flour, and sugar as I was always baking. I kept canned food on hand, along with oats, as we had a lot of people coming through to either help us or work for us. Hungry workers wanted three meals a day with morning and afternoon teas, and oh man, could they eat! The young fellows who worked in the mine sometimes shot rabbits or hares which I simmered until tender, then dipped in flour and deep fried ... mmm, delicious.

Our pastor, his wife and all the church youth came out for one long weekend. They bunked down in the units, which were fully equipped for self-sufficiency. On the Sunday morning we all went up the mountain for the sunrise, prayer, breakfast – everyone brought their own food – and then our morning service. It was a beautiful time. One woman shared a vision she'd received and gave the interpretation at church at Bowen that night. Brian and Jenny and the girls came out occasionally for the weekend and we'd fish in the creek. One day the fish were really biting; we caught sixty-two, so Cherie and Nicole started fishing, too. We had wonderful times out there. On the school holidays, the girls used to take it in turns to stay for a week which was best for me because I was working.

Friends of ours, farmers in Bowen, used to fly out often, particularly after they had been saved. We had told them so much about Jesus and what He had done in our lives that they wanted to know Him for themselves. Our friend took us to Daydream Island one day for a joy flight. We used to stay with them in Bowen and called their home our 'townhouse'. Other members of their family accepted Jesus because of their testimony of what He had done for them."

Ada at the Rutherford Table gold mine

Chapter 13

The time came when we had exhausted viability in our open-cut mining leases and didn't want to return to mining underground. Greg had left some time before to do mission work overseas and it was hard to get men to work underground and live in the same conditions as we were used to.

We sold the lease for the mine and the buyer paid the deposit with the balance due within twelve months, however, the money didn't come through in time. Fortunately, our solicitor had ensured that the contract stipulated that I held the mortgage on the leases, equipment and the goods and chattels until the balance was paid.

After that setback, we contacted a Rockhampton agent who acted for investors wanting to buy into gold mines. Our solicitor added further conditions to the mortgage contract; that the first buyer had to agree to the sale to the second buyer. The agent located another buyer from New Zealand who transferred the full amount to our account, when suddenly, the first buyer paid the outstanding balance. As the original buyer didn't agree to the second buyer we were in the clear legally and so the first buyer obtained ownership of the mine.[46] Therefore, we fully refunded the New Zealander.

Free at last, we drove south along the Queensland coast in search of our dream property. After twenty years in dry bush country, we wanted acreage where the land was lush and green. We also wanted a property with two dwellings because Brian and Jenny Smith, when they learned we were leaving Rutherford Table and moving south, said, "You're not going without us." We didn't find anything we could get excited about until we reached Gympie. With a creek and tropical bush frontage, cleared land in the middle and tall timbers on a hill at the back, the property at Wilson's Pocket was eighteen hectares of heaven on earth compared to what we had been used to. The main house looked a dump and needed work, which we knew we could do. The second dwelling was in a very poor state and needed a

---

46 Years later, we learned that the new owners of the mine abandoned it when the mine collapsed and buried the machinery I had built, because they had ignored my instructions that they restrict the width of the mine to three-and-a-half metres. Apparently, they had gone way beyond that and subsequently, suffered the consequences, almost losing their lives.

huge amount of work to make it livable. The owner really wanted to sell and the price was right. We saw that the property had a lot of potential as our retirement project.

Wilson's Pocket – a new beginning

After paying the deposit, we returned to the mine to pack up everything. We bought a prime mover and modified it for the job ahead. Greg was home at the time, so he and Brian helped transport our equipment, including the bulldozer, in three trips to Gympie.

Brian and Jenny moved to Wilson's Pocket with us for a while and it really was a happy family time. They prepared under the house to make it comfortable and Brian found work driving coaches. The girls were bussed to town for school. One day when Jenny was on her way to Gympie eighteen kilometres away, the fan belt broke on the car. The experience of being isolated and needing to deal with issues like this, helped her to realise that, at heart, she was not a country girl, so they bought a house in town. Rebuilding the second house on the property didn't eventuate until we prepared the property for sale years later.

We did a huge amount of work on our decrepit new home. We built a veranda and steps on the east side of the house to make a new entrance, painted both inside and outside and installed a new kitchen. We ran about twenty head of young cattle to keep the grass down, we had chooks, pigeons, quail, guinea fowl, two peacocks, ducks, dogs and various cats over time. As we didn't want to sit around twiddling our thumbs, we also planted an orchard, vegetable gardens and Ada's large ornamental garden. I cut a lot of timber from the property and milled it before the law changed which would have prohibited us from doing so.

Being retired gave us the time to spend with people and doing what we pleased. We often helped a couple who had young children and an orchard, by picking peaches and custard apples mainly, and packing the fruit. Ada also looked after their boys whenever needed.

After a couple of years, I developed shortness of breath and doctors wanted to run tests to diagnose the problem. Two days before my appointment, a visiting minister from Hawaii spoke at our church, and by a word of knowledge called out the person who had recently been diagnosed with a heart problem. I was the only one who responded to her invitation and she prayed for me. From memory, I didn't feel any instant relief. However, by the next day I knew I'd been healed.

The following day I attended my appointment with a specialist. I was put on a treadmill and wired up to the heart monitor. After a minute at walking normally, the speed was increased gradually until I was running. When the machine stopped, the practitioner said that I was in remarkable shape for my age. I replied, "You should have seen me a couple of days ago, I was a wreck." She asked what had changed. I replied, "I'm glad you asked. Someone prayed for me." She then asked quietly about the how, what, where and when regarding this prayer. The specialist, who was on the other side of the room, must have overheard our conversation, and remarked, "Thank God someone else is helping because we're overwhelmed with work." I was declared fit, not given any medication and returned home a happy man. Praise God!

At Wilson's Pocket one day as I walked about fifty metres down the paddock, my knee buckled, collapsed under me and dropped me on all fours to the ground. In the Name of Jesus I rebuked whatever had caused it to happen, picked myself up as I prayed in tongues, told the devil to leave and went merrily on my way. I used my authority as a believer in Jesus, the Healer, to deliver me from what appeared to be an attack from the enemy. I'd never had an issue with my knee before, although, in other places in my body I've had to stand against arthritis on a few occasions but I have always overcome it through prayer! Any answer to prayer is a miracle because it brings God's Kingdom will into our natural earthly realm.[47]

---

[47] "Your kingdom come. Your will be done on earth as it is in heaven." (Matthew 6:10)

**Shelley and Jeff
on their wedding day**

When I was 72, Shelley and Jeff were married. I had developed some health issues and required hospitalisation, so we were unable to go to Melbourne for their wedding. Being in hospital meant Ada was left alone on the farm; a future prospect she did not want to consider and, as her heart had been set on a move to town for some time, we decided to sell and buy in Gympie. We had lived at Wilson's Pocket for ten years and, when we sold, we received double what we had paid for the property. Clearly, God's blessing!

On the day of settlement in 2005 we still didn't have a new property in our sights nor anywhere to live in the interim, so we rented our property at Wilson's Pocket for a couple of weeks until we had a new home. We thought we had found just the one in Gympie (really, all I could see was its three sheds) but within an hour of that falling through, we noticed a 'For Sale' sign on another house, literally just up the road, inspected it, and confounded the owners when we offered to buy it and move in as soon as possible. Their sign had been up for only an hour. Having just been rejected as buyers of one home a stone's throw away, we saw clearly that the Lord had our new home organised ahead of us!

Wilson's Pocket – a lot of hard work later

After we moved in we built a shed, a garage, a big water tank, enlarged the dam, and planted trees, another orchard, vegetable gardens and ornamentals. Over time, Ada has accumulated a large collection of orchids due to a lot of birthday and Christmas gifts. And some are there just because I love her! We wanted to travel, so I converted a bus into a motor home and added a trailer to take a small vehicle with an aluminium boat over the top.

Our new home at Gympie

On Ada's eightieth birthday, Greg gave us a trip on a houseboat in Sandy Strait, near Hervey Bay. Ada wasn't too keen on the idea at first, as she really didn't enjoy boating due to past bad experiences. However, by the time we returned home she was wondering about a job as a houseboat cook! This led Greg and I to dream about buying a houseboat. He found one called *Jus*

Relaxin, at Jacob's Well. It needed an upgrade, so we made an offer lower than the asking price and it was accepted. We transported it to Tin Can Bay, where it is moored. We worked hard to get it up to regulation standard; putting in new motors, a green toilet and rebuilt the back end. It requires ongoing work to keep it up to specifications. Cleaning of mould and barnacles on the outside paintwork is a constant task. *Jus Relaxin* is our home away from home, from where we catch fish and mud crabs.

Jus Relaxin **at Tin Can Bay**

Gympie has been home for twenty years now and we love living there. Greg retired and lives with us, and Shelley and Jeff, also retired live up this way, too. We see Jenny and Brian and their family quite often. The Lord has given us grandchildren and a great-grandchild through them. We've found our place here, helped by our connection to a great Christian community.

The year 2021 marked our seventieth wedding anniversary and ninetieth birthdays. All praise to Jesus Christ, our Saviour and Lord, for His goodness and faithfulness to us for all these years!

At the end of February 2022, the Gympie area experienced the worst floods since 1894. We had to evacuate our flooded home at three o'clock in the morning. It was pitch black due to the electricity being out of action. Greg was away at the time, so he couldn't help us. I had a lot of things that I had packed on our dining table to take if it became necessary, but we never expected the flood waters to drive us out of our home. At half-past two, wading around in our darkened kitchen, shocked at the realisation that we had to leave, I said to Ada, "I have no idea how I'm going to get all this to the car." I had loaded some things into the car earlier and driven it to higher ground. Just then we heard a call from outside, "Do you need any help?" Three able-bodied men appeared out of the darkness and proceeded to carry out our belongings and guide us out of our home to safety. After we had been transported via boat to the evacuation centre, a wonderful Christian couple claimed us almost immediately and cared for us in their home until we could return to our property.

God is faithful to His Word: He will never forsake or leave us.[48] Nothing is impossible with our God![49]

I want to end my story by saying ...
I'm still in love with Ada! And she's sticking with me. By the way, she never did buy her own suitcase. And I can't remember if she paid back the money she borrowed to go to Carrathool!

The happy couple!

---

48 Deuteronomy 31:6
49 Luke 1:37

Where there is love the heart is light,
Where there is love the day is bright.
Where there is love there is a song,
To help when things are going wrong.
Where there is love there is a smile,
To make all things seem more worthwhile.
Where there is love there's a quiet peace,
A tranquil place where turmoils cease.
Love changes darkness into light,
And makes the heart take wingless flight.

Oh, blessed are they who walk in love,
They also walk with God above.
And when you walk with God each day
And kneel together when you pray,
Your marriage will be truly blessed
And God will be your daily Guest.
And love that once seemed yours alone
God gently blends into His Own.[50]

I'm praying that whoever reads this book, having been blessed and encouraged, will pass it on to others.

---

50 Attributed to Helen Steiner Rice.

If you do not know Jesus as your Saviour and Lord and you want to start a relationship with the living God, Romans chapter 10 verses 9-11 state, "And what is God's 'living message'? It is the revelation of faith for salvation, which is the message that we preach. For if you publicly declare with your mouth that Jesus is Lord and believe in your heart that God raised him from the dead, you will experience salvation. The heart that believes in Him receives the gift of the righteousness of God – and then the mouth confesses, resulting in salvation. For the Scriptures encourage us with these words: 'Everyone who believes in Him will never be disappointed'."[51]

Please pray this prayer of faith:
> God in Heaven, I confess that I have sinned against You and tried to live my life without You. I'm sorry and I turn away from living like that. I believe that Jesus died on the cross for me so that my sins would be forgiven. I believe that You raised Him from the dead and that He lives to intercede for me. I ask Your Holy Spirit to come into my heart and to be Lord of my life. From this moment on help me to live every day for You and in a way that pleases You. Thank You. Amen.

---
[51] Scripture reference from The Passion translation.

Next steps:
- Remember, salvation is by grace, through faith and is a free gift from God. There's nothing you did, or ever can do, to deserve it. All you have to do is receive it!
- Talk to God every day. You don't have to use big fancy words. There are no right and wrong words. Just be yourself. Thank the Lord daily for your salvation. Pray for others in need. Seek His direction. Ask Him daily to fill you with His Holy Spirit. You can pray with your eyes closed or open, while sitting or standing, kneeling or lying on your bed, anywhere, anytime.
- Read from the Bible every day to learn about the new life God has given you. A good place to start is the Book of Matthew in the New Testament.
- Find a Bible-believing church that ministers the power of Holy Spirit and connect to the community there.

Afterword

This book evolved over a five-year period. During a prophecy given to Shelley at our church in Victoria in 2019 she was asked, "do you write?" She was then told that she would write a book that would increase the faith of many people. This was right out of left field as she had never written anything like a book. Just six weeks later, while in conversation with her father, he mentioned that he'd love to record all the miracles God had done in their family's lives, but he wasn't a writer. In amazement, we realised God was leading us, via the prophecy and so we agreed to write her Dad's story.

As Des lived in Queensland, we attempted on two occasions to begin collating the stories over the phone. However, both times he became ill and was hospitalised, so the work was abandoned before it truly began. It seemed that some spiritual force didn't want the book written. Over time we encouraged him to list the stories with their details and we planned to compile the book from his notes.

Eventually, he completed the list, but then in February 2022 Gympie experienced its worst floods in 130 years and Shelley's parents had to evacuate their home. His notes were thought lost to the floodwaters. Eventually, in the clear out of their flooded home he found the sodden notes. He prised them apart, page by page and recovered all that he had written. Later that year Shelley sat each day for a week on their front verandah (the house was still gutted waiting repairs) and typed, while her Dad narrated from his recovered notes.

Mid 2023, we moved back to Queensland permanently and worked on the book to the place where we felt it was ready for publication. Though it's been a dislocated literary journey our part in the prophecy has been fulfilled. Therefore, may your faith in the God Who does miracles be increased!

Shelley and Jeff Reaney
February 2025

Acknowledgement

The writers wish to acknowledge G I Morton,
former pastor of Des and Ada who wrote the book,
Miracles Beyond the Black Stump (now out of print)
about the many miracles they experienced
in their first ten months as Christians.
Some parts of his book have been used or
adapted in the writing of our book.

Close the Gates

by Jeff Reaney

Many people wonder why they can't live the kind of life they aspire to. Despite their best efforts at leading a good life, misfortunes still afflict them. Christians, just like anyone else, suffer mental or physical illnesses and sad events like marital breakdown, despite following Biblical teachings.

In this book, Jeff Reaney asserts that deceptive spiritual forces take advantage of family conflict, dysfunctional relationships, rejection and all kinds of abuse to manipulate our emotions and control our actions. He lifts the lid on ways spiritual predators use seemingly benign activities, past events, illnesses and even our thoughts to control and plunder our lives.

Drawing on a wealth of personal experience, this practical book explains the necessity of accepting individual responsibility, the power of forgiveness and the use of spiritual authority against these forces. Learn how to evict these opportunistic predators by bringing closure to past mistakes and hurtful events, enjoy freedom and peace, and step into the fullness of your destiny.

Enquiries regarding purchasing this book can be directed to
reaneyj@yahoo.com
The author also conducts seminars titled
Closing the Gates: Understanding the Demonic Realm,
the material of which is based largely on the book.
He is also available for personal consultations.

www.ingramcontent.com/pod-product-compliance
Lightning Source LLC
Chambersburg PA
CBHW071853070526
44583CB00016B/1673